Cedar Fish Campground Map

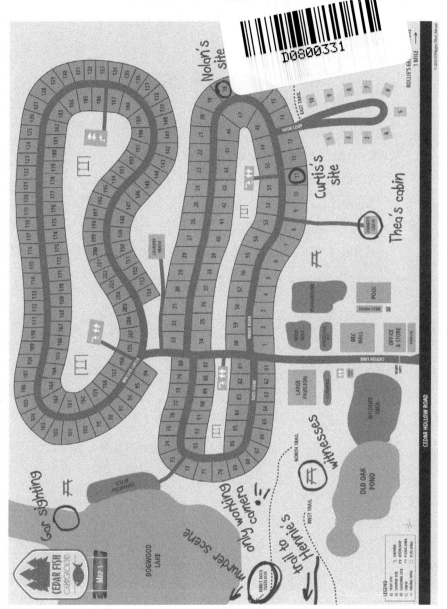

Books by Zoey Chase

Cedar Fish Campground Series
Book 1: Between a Rock and a Deadly Place
Book 1.5: Fishy Beginnings
Book 2: Breath of Fatal Air
Book 3: One Body Short of a Picnic

BETWEEN A ROCK AND A DEADLY PLACE

BETWEEN A ROCK AND A DEADLY PLACE

CEDAR FISH CAMPGROUND SERIES: BOOK ONE

Leslie,
Welcome to
cedar Fish
campground!
Enjoy your
stay!

Zoey Chase

PAGES THAT *move*

PaGes THaT
move
Pittsburgh, PA
www.PagesThatMove.com

Printed in the United States of America

First Edition, 2019

ISBN 978-1-951873-01-1

Visit www.ZoeyChase.com and join my mailing
list for freebies, occasional updates, and new
release information.

Keftedakia and Sauce Recipe

Did your mouth water like Nolan's over the keftedakia?
Get the recipe for **Thea's Keftedakia and Sauce**
FREE when you join my mailing list!

Get a Cedar Fish Campground Full-Color Map!

Marked with important locations from book one:

- Murder Scene
- Witness Location
- Only Working Camera
- Thea's Cabin
- Nolan's Campsite
- Curtis's Campsite
- Gar Sighting
- Trail to Hennie's

---

www.ZoeyChase.com/freebies

For Jonathan:

You've given me more love, grace, and support than I knew a human could. None of this would be possible without you.

CHAPTER 1

The demanding voice from my phone sounded warbled through the monsoon pounding my car's roof. I blinked at the road ahead, but the fog from my panicked breath had crept up the windshield. I flicked on my turn signal—not that anyone would be stupid enough to be driving out there to see it—and eased onto the shoulder.

I stared at my phone. It chimed, "Rerouting..." and with the percussive storm, it came out like a chorus. "Rerouting... Rerouting..."

I shoved my phone into the console space, smashing a collection of metallic chip bags and gum wrappers. The drive had felt long, and I'd been over it two hours and a hundred miles ago. Somewhere on the random crap pile beside me, I had a map. I moved a desk lamp, a Crockpot lid, and my purse so I could grab a corner and yank the map into view.

The amber light of my fuel gauge glared back at me. Since I'd hit the outer limits of Branson, gas stations had become scarce. That should have been an indication that people in this part of Missouri didn't drive as much as they did back in St. Louis, but judging from the sheer size of this county, people would have to drive ages to get anywhere.

The map was little help. The lines all looked wrong and didn't match the image in my mind. I tried to shake free ten years of memory dust to get back to my twenty-six-year-old self—the last self that had been to the campground. I looked again at the road lines and my pencil markings.

I adjusted my heat and mirrors, waited for the fog to clear from my windows, and crept back onto the road. After a few more miles, I saw a familiar site, and my heart skipped. A glowing sign boasted, "Rollie's." The general store was just a mile from the campground.

Memories poured over me as I passed the log-cabin style building. I'd gone in there with my grandad and grandma too many times to count. The pang hit my chest again, and I swallowed hard. *No*, I reminded myself. *I'm not doing grief on this drive—I am saving that for later.*

I had to get to the campground, and as soon as possible. My dashboard clock flickered as the time bumped up. Another minute gone. But what was one more on top of the forty minutes I was already late?

I pressed on the gas as I rounded the bend, but quickly shifted to the brake when I saw the debris. I clenched my teeth as the car jolted to a stop. Fine line between slamming the brake hard enough to slide and not hard enough to keep me from smashing into the tree that blocked the road.

This had to be the beginning of a horror story: lone woman in a storm is trapped when a tree blocks her path, and she can't escape because she's out of gas and has no cell service. I stared the tree down through the rain. There would be no getting around it. No getting through it. Definitely no moving it. Any sort of power saw I might have access to waited beyond the blockade. I'd have no clue how to use it anyhow. *Sorry, Grandad.* Never did get into power tools.

Fallen trees weren't all that uncommon in the Ozarks. Once, when I was just six or seven, I'd been with Grandad, talking to old Rollie himself. We'd hopped into Grandad's old pickup to head back to the campground and had come upon a fallen tree, much like I faced now. We'd backed right up, turned around, and had taken the long way to the campground. Of course, Grandad had then taken his chainsaw down to the tree and cut it up to clear the road. We'd had a nice bonfire once the wood dried.

After my three-point-turn, I made two lefts, followed the curving road for an extra three miles, and finally saw the sign.

An arc of words reading, "Cedar Fish Campground," stretched over a carved, wooden fish. My throat tightened as I recalled watching Grandad carve that fish. I still found it hard to believe the campground belonged to me now.

The weight of the honor and the responsibility sat heavily on my heart.

I turned in and parked in front of the office. With my rain jacket yanked over my head, I dashed to the door where a note had been taped. Unfortunately, the office's front overhang had not protected the door in the storm. The note was wet and its words badly smudged. I made out my name—Thea—above "ome" and "ollie's" and eventually figured out that the small smudge between the words was "to."

Normally, it would be a quick drive down the road to Rollie's, but I'd have to take the long way again—twice in order to get back. Irritation slithered up my neck. Yes, I was late. I couldn't blame Enid for not waiting, especially in this storm. But now I'd spend at least another half hour in the car when I just wanted to eat, stretch my legs, and get dry. Had I known she wasn't here, I would have stopped at Rollie's the first time I passed it.

I slammed my car into reverse and squeezed the gas. Rather than go around the gate to get to the exit, I drove the wrong way out of the entrance. I heard the loud hiss as my car halted. Right. The tire spikes.

I reached for my cup of ice and threw my head back to receive its contents, but only a few drops of water hit my tongue. A low growl rumbled in my throat as I jammed the cup back into the holder.

Well. At least now I could take the shorter route. I dug under my seat for my umbrella and yanked my purse up my arm. I hadn't thought to keep a flashlight handy. I paused before getting out. Maybe it would be better to stay in one of the cabins tonight. Except all the keys would be inside the locked office. It was either sleep in the car and eat chips for dinner or brave the storm.

With my jacket zipped and hood up, I pushed out of the car, clutching my umbrella as I hurried through the rain in the dark. Fear churned in my stomach. Alone like this, anything could happen. I took in long, deep breaths, trying to keep myself calm. What had my therapist said? Not every place is dangerous. And that's why I'd come. To find a safer place. To find a Russell-free place.

I shivered and picked up my pace. When I reached the downed tree, I found a spot low enough to step over. My fingers were numb and my clothes were damp by the time I saw the light of Rollie's welcoming me. I trudged up three stairs and pushed open the creaking door, nearly tripping over the large dog lying just inside.

The old golden retriever didn't move as I stepped over him. I folded my umbrella and set it by the door where it quickly formed a puddle. I looked around nervously.

"Oh, don't you worry about that," a voice called to me. "Come on over here, dear, my goodness."

I turned, searching for the person who spoke. "Hello?"

"Here, honey."

I took a few steps forward. In front of me stood tall, wooden shelves filled with boxed food and goods. On the wall to the left, a sign read, "Post Office." On the other side of the building it said, "Bank." The far wall, which sat in shadow, said, "Bar." Strange but convenient collection.

I moved toward a shuffling sound in the next aisle, passing a row of muffin mixes and baking supplies until I saw the source of the sound. A very large turtle made its way down the aisle. It might've come inside to seek shelter from the storm, but the diaper around its back legs told me otherwise.

"There you are."

I let out a squeal as I jumped and spun. "Oh. Hi." I stuck out my hand.

The woman ignored my hand and pulled me into a crushing hug.

"I'm all wet," I protested.

"No bother when it's been so long since I've seen you!" She patted my cheeks with soft, wrinkled hands and squinted a smile at me. "Oh, little Thea, returned at last."

I blinked at the woman who had to be in her 90s. She had a well-weathered face with deep laugh lines, framed by wisps of white hair that had fallen from her messy bun. She wore a long, navy skirt and a cardigan sweater covered in purple and yellow triangles—a pattern only my carefree, spirited grandma could have pulled off. Well, they had been best friends for something like fifty years. Must've rubbed off on each other.

"Enid." I took her hands in mine, and my smile was genuine. "It's good to see you, too."

"Let's get you warmed up while you tell me all about that big city of yours."

I laughed. "It's not mine anymore."

"Of course not, dear. You're a Fisher at heart, even if you're a Pagoni by name."

"Blame my mother for that one," I said.

She took my hand and led me to a back room. The little space smelled dusty with age. Boxes of toilet paper and paper towels lined one wall, and a small table with two folding chairs sat against the other. A refrigerator hummed in the corner. A Crockpot sat on the cluttered counter near the sink. My mouth watered at the warm, spicy scent of chili.

"It's been here all day, but it'll still be good, I promise." Enid scooped some into a bowl and set it on the table, then dug a plastic spoon from a box.

I didn't even thank her or bother to sit before shoving a steaming spoonful into my mouth. The burn was evidence that heat existed in the world, and it was mine for the taking. The heat traveled down my throat and through my chest, warming me. I took two more bites before looking up at her.

"You're an angel."

She waved me off. "Soon enough, dear. Soon enough." She sat in the other chair, facing me. "Tell me all about this big city life you've been living."

I let out a long breath. "Not much to tell. After everything that happened with Russell, I couldn't stand St.

Louis anymore. Grandma's passing was terrible timing in some ways—one more tragedy on top of everything else. But, weirdly, it was also perfect. Cedar Fish was always a quiet escape for me. I was looking for a way to leave the law firm, and this was the perfect opportunity."

Enid patted my hand. "That husband of yours..." She shook her head. "Your grandmother told me horrible things."

"*Ex*-husband. And they're probably all true."

She leaned in conspiratorially. "I hope your lawyer made him pay you good for all he did to you."

"Yeah..." I gritted my teeth hard enough to make my jaw ache.

The last thing I wanted to discuss was how my ex had ruined me financially and all the ways my divorce lawyer had failed me.

My fist tightened and I forced it to release as I took another bite of chili.

"So... is business good?" I hadn't seen any cars or customers, but with the weather, that didn't tell me much.

"I get by." Enid handed me a steaming mug. "Thea, your grandmother would flip if she knew I gave you hot cocoa from a packet."

I chuckled as I wrapped my hands around the mug. Tears filled my eyes. "Yeah. She would."

We exchanged sorrowful gazes and then she forced a smile. "Well, she'll never know."

We chuckled, and the sadness melted along with the iciness from my fingers.

"You'll have your work cut out for you, I'm afraid," Enid said. "We did our best, ole Bettie and me, but we just couldn't keep up with everything."

I nodded. "The lawyer said the campground needed some TLC."

Enid's eyes widened. "*Some.*" She tsked then pulled an envelope from her cardigan pocket. "This is for you."

Inside, I found a collection of keys and index cards filled with various codes, passwords, and combinations.

"Of course, you can ask me anything," Enid said. "And you'll have Curtis. He's been there a long time. He's pretty handy."

"Thanks. I hope you're right, because my car is blocking the entrance." I took my final sip of cocoa and set the mug down. "And my front tires are flat."

She nodded in understanding. "I'll have our bartender drive you and move it. He's not doing anything over there anyhow in this weather."

"That would be fabulous."

I followed Enid to the bar and hugged her goodbye before walking outside with a tall man who she introduced as Arlo. He took me in his SUV around the long way to the campground. He wasn't bad looking, seemed friendly, and was probably in his late thirties like me, but my heart did not react to him. With a recent and painful divorce, romance wasn't something I could consider.

Arlo pulled his hood up to avoid the rain as he pushed my car into a parking spot while I steered. I thanked him and saw him off before walking to my cabin—my new home.

I dug through the keys for the correct one and opened the door. My heart stuck in my throat when I saw that the place looked exactly as I remembered. The small living room where Grandma would read us stories was off to the right, across from the kitchen where I'd eaten countless meals. A staircase I'd thundered up and down with my sister separated the rooms, leading upstairs, where two bedrooms were located. I'd spent the night in the smaller room many times with my sister, parents, and various cousins and other family members, crammed into one of many bunk beds or in a sleeping bag on the floor. On occasion, there were so many of us that we spilled into the living room.

The sofa was still the faded green with tiny dots of cream that I remember tracing my fingertips over endlessly on rainy days. I touched the fabric, feeling the familiar bumps of soft white. The smell was the same. Lingering garlic and fried onions—the smell of my grandmother's divine cooking. On the round table at the edge of the kitchen sat the old crystal vase that had been a wedding gift to my grandad and grandma more than seventy years ago. How did such a vase last so long in a place like this?

I took my overnight bag upstairs into the forbidden larger bedroom. We'd been told over and over—do not go into Grandad and Grandma's room. Ever. Now it was my room, but I still felt a thrill of defiance as I entered it.

I set my bag on the white-ruffled bedspread and the tears ran down my face. I sat down and listened to the rain on the roof as I allowed myself a moment of grief for my grandparents.

CHAPTER 2

That first morning, I woke to the sound of birds chirping and a rooster hollering. I lay in bed for several luxurious moments, taking in the pure peacefulness of it. Anxiety seemed to melt from my chest as the noise and chaos of the city faded from my mind. Here, the solitude made me feel safe.

I sucked up a deep breath and stretched as I got out of bed, rubbing the sore spot in my lower back. Had to be from driving for five hours and the burden of moving and carrying things I didn't normally carry.

Overnight bag in hand, I walked to the bathroom and took a quick shower, noting how the grout needed to be scrubbed and that I needed to figure out why the water had a brown tint. After drying off and finishing my bathroom routine, I reached automatically for my makeup bag, but paused. Did I really need it out there in the woods? Who was I trying to impress, the raccoons?

I left the makeup bag and pulled my dark hair into a ponytail. With my old sneakers laced tight, long-ago-broken-in jeans hanging off my waist, and my favorite grey hoodie pulled over my head, I bounced down the stairs and found the only box I'd brought inside in the downpour. I took out my pen and notebook, made sure my phone was in my back pocket, and stepped outside into the dewy spring morning.

From my cabin, I had a fairly good view of the front of the campground. The original owners had planned it that way—that the owner's home should be able to get a quick glimpse of anything going on near the office, front gate, rec hall, or pool area.

When I'd pulled in last night, it had been dark, and the rain had obscured the scenery. I'd also been in a hurry and starving. I hadn't taken a good look at things, assuming my memory would be an accurate picture of Cedar Fish Campground. I was wrong.

Most of the grounds were overgrown, as if they hadn't been mowed yet this year. The combination office and store building, which was sided in wooden boards, boasted large sections of peeling paint and sections with no paint at all. The wood looked rotted in many places. The roof, too, was spotted with dark patches of decay amongst the shingles that had parted ways long ago. The rec hall building, which had always been a lively place full of crafts or music, seemed just as dilapidated with its broken window that had been repaired with duct tape.

My stomach tightened as I took in the pool. In my mind, it was bright blue and filled with crystal water. The pool now was a murky green bath of slime and mud. The walls appeared to still be some shade of blue, though the paint had faded and cracked in places.

Of the 60 camper sites, only three of the seasonals contained a stored camper. And it looked like their inhabitants hadn't arrived yet for the season. What I could see of the 207 tent sites spread over a hundred acres of land sat nearly empty. I counted a handful of tent sites in use, but knew that when the place was booked, tents of all colors dotted the hillside. Grandad, in all his cleverness, always joked that the colors were *in-tents*. Insert eye roll here.

What was intense was the pure weight of desolation I felt hovering over the grounds. My once-treasured adventure land had fallen to ruin.

A small wave of panic clawed at the edges of my chest. What if this had been a mistake? What if this failed horribly?

I forced myself to breathe slowly. It was all fixable. Of course the campers were sparse in the off season. Memorial Day weekend was still a month away. After that, the seasonal section would be populated, and the sites would be full. In the meantime, I would get things cleaned up and ready. I just needed a plan.

The boxes still in my car seemed like the perfect task to accomplish quickly to gain a sense of achievement. It was a trick I learned in my law days to help me feel ready to tackle something difficult. Play a round or two of Candy Crush, and the small boost of confidence it gave me would be enough to get me moving.

My trunk and backseat contained everything I had brought along from the city. I'd purposely restricted myself to one carload to force me to purge. Though, somehow I'd managed to bring along far too many shoes. I pulled the "shoe" box from my trunk and carried it inside. The rest of the boxes made their way to my kitchen, bathroom, living room, or bedroom. It didn't take as long as I thought, and I did feel a glimmer of satisfaction in having crossed something off my list.

With my laptop bag over my shoulder, I snatched up my notebook, turned to a blank page, and stepped off my porch to get a better assessment of the campground's damages. By the time I reached the office, I had a decent-sized list. It continued to grow as I entered the building.

Lights dusty and dim. Old items on shelves collecting dust—literally. Dated flyers, dingy floors, disheveled fishing poles for sale. I shook my head and jumped when the man behind the front counter coughed.

"Oh! I didn't see you there!" I approached him, assuming this hunched over, white-haired man was Curtis, my only employee.

He cleared his throat for a long time. Then cleared it once more. "Nice to meet you, Ms. Pagoni."

"Thea is just fine." I set my bag on the counter and stuck my hand out to him.

He lifted his slowly. Inch by inch, his hand crept toward mine, and when I finally took hold, I had to be extra careful not to squeeze.

"Do you usually run the front desk?" I asked.

He nodded slowly. "And fix things."

It didn't seem to me that he could fix a peanut butter and jelly sandwich. So much for the handyman Enid had promised.

"What's your usual schedule?" I would have to get a feel for our busy times and assess our employee coverage.

"Most days, I head over after breakfast and then home around dinner time."

"Do you live nearby?"

He nodded. "Site 11."

He must be one of our seasonal campers who lived in the campground year-round. "Do you know of any auto repair shops close by? I need new tires for my car."

He squinted at me through the thick lens of his glasses. "New tires?"

"In the storm, I didn't see the tire spikes and drove over them."

Curtis slid off the stool with care and took two shuffling steps. I watched him creep toward the end of the counter.

I started with, "Umm...?" but wasn't sure what to ask.

He stopped and turned to look at me.

"So, do you know a repair shop or...?"

"I'm going to get the tires. We have some in the storage shed and I'll get them put on for you."

"Oh, I..." What were the chances we had two spare tires that fit my car and were in good condition? Beyond that, what were the chances Curtis would survive attempting the repair? "That's okay. Whatever tires are there belong to the campground. I'll just search online."

He stared at me a moment, then shuffled back to his stool.

I noticed a flashing red light on the front counter's phone. "Is that a voicemail message?"

Curtis squinted and leaned closer until I thought he might topple off the stool. I raised my hand instinctively in case he started to tip.

"Yes," he said.

"Do you know how to check it?"

He took ages to shuffle back over to the phone, picked it up, held it to his ear, then pressed the button beside the flashing light. He handed the phone to me.

"Message received on December 23 at 1:51 a.m." I grabbed a pen to take notes but hesitated over the date. Had this message really been sitting there for almost four months? The time seemed off, too.

"Hi, I'm wondering about your hiking trails," the voice said. I struggled to determine if the person was male or female. There was a feminine sounding sigh, but the voice was gruff.

"I need to know which ones have tall cliffs. I called before, but no one called me back. When are you open?"

I gritted my teeth as the message ended. She hadn't even left her name or number so that I could return the call.

I hung up. "How do I check the date and time?"

Curtis took the phone from me and dialed a series of numbers, then handed it back.

When I held it to my ear, I heard, "At the tone, the time in Central Daylight Time will be..."

I set the phone back down with a heavy sigh. "What I meant was, the message said it was from this past December at 2 a.m., which I'm guessing isn't correct. Do these messages get checked every day?"

He nodded slowly.

"Do you know how to check the time of the messaging system so that I can fix it?"

He pulled his overgrown eyebrows together and stared at me. The moment stretched on for so long that I took the answer to be no.

"I'll figure it out." I shifted the logbook on the counter so I could read it. "Is this what we're taking reservations in?"

Curtis nodded and lifted his chest. "Been doing it that way for fifty years."

"Is... that how long you've worked here?"

He looked up at me with an expression I thought was confusion. I couldn't recall any Curtis when I spent summers there in my childhood. I shrugged and flipped through the empty pages.

"Where are all the bookings?"

He turned a few pages, stopped to lick his thumb, turned a few more pages, squinted at the date at the top of the page, and turned another page. One hand-written entry was listed for July. A few more scattered through August. According to today's log, we had only five sites full. I knew there were a lot of walk-ins, but that couldn't be right.

"Where are the rest?"

"That's it so far."

I frantically turned page after page. Blank, blank, blank. My heart rate spiked.

"Do we have a soda machine or ice machine?"

Curtis lifted a shaky hand and pointed toward an ice chest in the corner of the store. "Not sure how much ice is in it, though."

I trudged over to the ice chest and opened the door. I expected a wave of cold air to hit me, but almost suffocated in the rush of warm staleness. On the floor of the cooler sat two empty bags and a stagnant puddle.

I gritted my teeth until the pain radiated into my jaw. As I walked back to the counter, I saw packs of gum and grabbed one, stuffing a minty piece into my mouth as quickly as I could. I chewed hard and glared at the list in my notebook.

A shadow streaked across the floor, and I shrieked as I jumped back. A soft *meow* came from the next aisle over and I relaxed. The cat peeked its tortoise-shell head around the counter and blinked at me.

"Dill!" I put out my hand, and she trotted to me, happily rubbing against my hand. "I can't believe you're still alive, old girl." I had been there the summer Dill was born. She must be pushing sixteen or seventeen by now. I finished petting her before continuing to assess the damage.

A dark green Subaru pulled up in front of the office. A young woman somewhere in her twenties got out, then entered the building. Though she wore sneakers and bright purple athletic pants, she didn't appear too fit. Her brown hair was in a ponytail at the back of her head and her upper lip looked stuck in a snarl.

"What time does the hiking trail open?" she demanded.

"Hi there," I said. "The trails are available dawn to dusk."

"And how long are they?"

I thought back. To my child's legs, those trails were hours long, but that couldn't be accurate. I looked to Curtis and he shrugged.

"I believe they're each several miles," I said.

She put her hand on her hip. "Well, can you find out for sure? I'm not going out there for no ten-mile hike. It's bad enough I have to go out there at all."

"Uhh... let me check." I rifled around the paperwork near the cash register. How wrong would it be to lie to her? "I'm sorry. I'm the new owner and this is my first day. I don't have that information right now, but I can tell you that the west trail is the shortest."

"West. Great." She rolled her eyes. "How about a cold drink?"

I grimaced. "Sorry. But that's a great idea. I'll have to get a vending machine for cold drinks." I jotted it down.

"But you don't have any now."

"No, I'm sorry."

She huffed and glared at me. "Ice cream?"

"Yes," I said excitedly, then recalled that in my initial walkthrough, I'd seen only a handful of ice cream options in the cooler beside the icebox.

I pointed, and she walked over to look through the transparent lid at the selections. "This place is awesome," she said sarcastically and walked out, letting the door shut hard behind her.

I stared after her a moment before adding "ice cream" to my list of things to research.

I told Curtis, "I'm going to walk around and take notes. Where are the walkie talkies?"

He dug under the counter for so long that the panic crept up from my chest, tightening my throat. I walked back there myself, and in the mess of clutter, I managed to locate one walkie talkie. One dead walkie talkie. A few more minutes of searching did not reveal the charger, so I instead tore a sheet of paper from a small notepad by the phone. I scribbled my cell number.

"If you need anything, I always have my phone on me."

I hurried out of the building before I started hyperventilating. In the cool morning breeze, I felt better. I sucked in greedy mouthfuls of freshness, the brisk country air scrubbing my lungs clean.

I took my time walking through the campground. I hadn't been there in ten years, and it was good to see familiar places. The small wildlife area still had its ducks, deer, goats, and chickens. The little bridge over Old Oak Pond was charming as ever, though decaying. The fishing dock at the edge of Dogwood Lake, where I'd spent long hours with Grandad, still called to me.

But the bathrooms sorely needed to be cleaned and repaired. None of the few cameras around the campground seemed to be working. The washing machines and dryers in the laundry house were questionable, and some of the play areas didn't look safe. Even the campsites themselves were overrun with brush and debris. Every square inch of the place would have to be addressed. My head pounded and I wished again that I had ice to chomp on.

I returned to the office, but this time, took my laptop into the smaller private office that was now mine. My computer connected to the Wi-Fi but took a while to locate the number of an auto repair shop. Once it did, I arranged for someone to come and change my tires. I'd have to keep in mind that the closest mechanic was twenty miles away.

Next, I wrote a simple ad for a handyman and called the local paper to place it.

Any day now, I'd get an email from Grandma and Grandad's lawyer, telling me what the final estate was after costs and fees and taxes. And that amount, however great or small, would be all I had to get the place fixed up and ready for the season. My gut twisted and my mind picked at the thing I didn't want to awaken. I sucked in a breath, but the rage shot through my chest anyway. My loaded savings account—years of banking chunks of a corporate lawyer's salary—plenty of money to turn Cedar Fish around and make it the place it should be. Gone. Every dollar out the door. Each screaming Russell's name. My fingernails dug into my palms.

I forced my eyes closed and counted ten breaths. My therapist's voice echoed between the numbers. *It's gone. You can't get it back. The anger won't bring it back. Your anger won't affect your ex, but it will affect you.*

I heard Russell's voice, his lies playing unbidden through my mind. *It's a solid investment. You can look over the paperwork yourself and see that we can't go wrong. I'll make our money back and then some. Trust me.* I never had gotten a copy of any paperwork. By the time I'd figured out that the first investment failed, he'd already moved onto another—that he neglected to tell me about until I saw the large withdrawal from the savings account.

I might have had a few dollars left from what he hadn't managed to blow, but my divorce lawyer had been expensive—and terrible. Russell was able to prove that I had supported him in the initial investment with evidence of my signature on the withdrawal form. Somehow, the fact that it was missing from all the other chunks of money he took out hadn't mattered. Since he'd quit his job to take on these ventures and had been out of work for so many years—again with my supposed approval—he was eligible for spousal support payments for two years. He was also awarded the majority of the remainder of the savings account since he so readily gave me the house. Only to later reveal, once the divorce agreement had been signed, that he'd forged my name on a second mortgage. Somehow my lawyer had missed it in the listing of debts.

I had grounds to sue. My background as a corporate lawyer would have aided me in getting back some of what had been taken from me. But by the time the divorce was finalized and the criminal case had been thrown out for a procedural violation during Russell's arrest, I'd had enough and so had my body. After multiple panic attacks and many therapy sessions to deal with not only the divorce, but the physical attack I'd suffered at Russell's hands, I knew when Grandma passed that I had to get out. It was worth my sanity to give up the fight. Only now, that decision had left me in an awful position to get things in the campground going.

I repeated my breathing exercises twice more before I got my heart rate to settle and the fire to clear from my mind. There was peace here. There was safety and healing here.

I refocused and got back to work. Whatever came through in the estate would have to be enough. I didn't know if I could actually afford to hire a handyman, but I had no choice. Curtis wouldn't be able to complete much of anything on my ever-growing list.

The bookings were another problem. Had reservations died off because the place was in such bad condition, or had the place gone into disrepair because the income had dried up? It would take some analysis, but the business end of things was one area I could handle. My years of law school and more years of working hard to make partner at a corporate law firm would not go to waste. All that knowledge would now go into saving this campground.

One of the first things I had to complete was an inventory. I grabbed my notebook again and walked through the store, writing down items and their quantities. The phone rang as I was counting packages of napkins. And kept ringing. After the fourth ring, I dashed to the front counter, reached past a napping Curtis, and picked up the phone.

"Cedar Fish Campground, how can I help you?" My first official call.

"Yeah, your tent sites? How much are they?" a man asked.

"I'd be glad to go over pricing with you." I searched for the latest flyer and pulled it.

"Do they all have water and electric?"

"The tent sites just have water. You'd need a camper site for electric."

"And how much is that?"

I went over all the price options and ended with, "Did you want to make a reservation?" I hope I didn't sound too eager.

"Oh no. That's all. Thanks."

The phone clicked, and I hung up with a disappointed sigh. Curtis snored and snapped his head up.

"What?" he croaked.

I pressed my lips together and sighed. "There was a phone call."

He picked up the phone and held it to his ear. "Hello?"

"No, I already took the call."

He hung up, adjusted himself on the stool, then closed his eyes again.

Just as I was considering how cruel it would be to fire him versus how much money was being wasted paying him, the little bell over the door jingled and I looked up.

In the doorway, with the bright sunlight behind her, the woman facing me looked huge. She stepped inside the store carrying a large cardboard box, which she promptly dropped at her feet. In the light, I saw she was shorter than me, maybe 5'2" at most.

"You the new one?" she barked.

Irritation flared in my chest. "I'm the new owner, yes. Thea Pagoni."

"Hennie Schrute." The woman nodded her head of frizzy grey hair. Several pieces had come loose from her messy braid and stuck out in random directions. Her button-up flannel shirt looked clean, but her tall galoshes were covered in mud. Which was now all over my floor.

"Can I help you?" I asked.

"Got the new order."

"Of?"

She picked up the box and brought it to me. When I didn't reach for it, she shoved it at me so I had to take it. Inside sat rows of jars, wrapped soaps, and rolled beeswax candles. I set the box down and picked up a jar of honey. I knew from my inventory list that we still had several jars on the shelf.

"I'm sorry, I don't think we can accept this order. We still have honey from the last order and—"

"What do you mean you can't accept it? It's your order."

The phone rang and I looked over at Curtis. It rang again.

"I understand that—" I clapped twice. "Curtis! Phone!"

He jumped and snatched the phone to his ear.

I tried again. "I'm sorry that—"

"No, I don't think you understand," the woman said. "This is your order."

I sucked in a long breath. "I understand that someone placed this order—"

"Well, it doesn't sound like you do."

Curtis hung up the phone but hadn't written anything down. He slid off the stool.

"Curtis? Everything okay?" I asked.

He held up a shaking finger as he moved to the end of the counter.

The woman continued. "See, Hennie's Honey has always been sold here, along with all of my other products. Regulars have come to expect it. They stock up, you know. Take it home to have all year until they come back. You can't just stop—"

I held up a hand. "I'll be real honest. From one business woman to another. This campground isn't doing too hot, in case you didn't notice. I can't afford to buy more products when my existing ones haven't sold. If you want to leave them on consignment, I'll consider working something—"

"Consignment! This is unacceptable. Curtis! Will you explain to this woman how it works?"

"This woman? I am the owner now, thank you."

Curtis stopped and looked at us. "I need to see about this call first."

"What was the call?" I asked.

"Someone out hiking. Said he found a dead girl on the trail."

CHAPTER 3

"What was that?" I asked Curtis. I must've heard him wrong. The fates couldn't hate me that much.

"Dead body," he repeated, still shuffling toward the door.

I looked at Hennie, whose eyes grew three sizes. "Well now, that's one way to start things off with a bang." At the word "bang" she pointed her finger like a gun and took a pretend shot in the air.

"Who called?" I asked.

"Young man."

"Where did he find...?"

"On the north trail."

Then I realized what he must've meant by body. "What kind of animal was it?"

"No animal, Miss Thea. A *girl*," he said with great emphasis.

I shook my head. "But that's not possible."

"You calling Curtis a liar?" Hennie squinted at me hard.

"No. I mean, it's too unbelievable."

"Curtis knows what he's talking about."

"Well, if it's true, then we have to call the cops. Curtis, stay inside please. We can't go near the body and take the chance of disturbing the accident scene."

"How do you know it was an accident?" Hennie raised an eyebrow.

I choked on the air in my lungs. "Because."

She waited.

I blurted, in a near-hysterical tone, "Because there is no way a murder took place in my grandparent's campground the very first day I take it over, when I moved my whole life to come here and do this, and when I've already lost everything!" My hands had tightened into fists, and I forced them open.

Hennie gave me an understanding nod.

I walked to the phone on the counter, breathing away the anxiety that chewed at my insides. I dialed 9-1-1 and explained as calmly and as clearly as I could, "This is Thea Pagoni from Cedar Fish Campground. We received a call that someone found a dead girl on one of our hiking trails."

"A dead girl?" Even the dispatcher didn't believe it.

"We haven't confirmed that, but that was the call, yes." I did my best to give her directions to our location.

"I'll dispatch police immediately, but the closest station is about twenty minutes away."

"Thank you." I hung up and stared at Hennie and Curtis. "We have to make sure no one else goes down that trail until the police arrive. Curtis, can you watch for the cops and direct them when they get here?"

He nodded.

"I'll grab my shotgun," Hennie said.

I followed her out the door and to her four-wheeler, where she picked up a shotgun from the back rack. She pumped it and aimed. "I'll stop anyone who tries to tamper with our crime scene."

"Accident scene," I corrected, "And I don't think deadly force will be necessary."

"What if the murderer shows up?"

"It's not a murder."

"Well, I'll be ready just in case."

We walked toward the north trail's entrance, past the rec hall and horseshoe pit, past the large pavilion. At the start of the gravel path, a sign read "North Trail - 3 miles." Below the sign, a thin metal box on a stand housed the trail's logbook. A few hundred feet of the trail could be seen before it disappeared into the woods. The late morning sun peeked through the trees, sending golden sun rays to dot the trail, making it look eerily welcoming.

My lawyer brain tapped at its cage as we waited. I let the door open briefly, and a rush of questions tumbled in. How had it happened? Had anyone seen it happen? Who was responsible for the accident? Did we have waivers or signs posted saying the campground wasn't liable for hiking accidents? Did we even have proper insurance to cover this sort of thing? So many charges could be applied, and I didn't want to consider the implications if somehow it was a crime. I shivered and looked again toward the main entrance.

When the police finally arrived—a frightening many minutes later—my shock at the response time was further aggravated by Hennie's comment: "They got here quick!" She lowered her gun as I waved the cops over.

An officer waddled toward us, adjusting the belt around his rotund middle with each step. A thinner, but no more competent-looking officer with messy brown hair and zero muscle left the cruiser and caught up to his partner.

"Officer Toby Randall." The tubby one stuck his hand out to me. "You the one who called?"

"Yes. I'm the owner."

The other officer also shook my hand. "Officer Reggie Longshore. You new to town?"

"I just arrived last night."

"Thought so." Officer Longshore ran his tongue over his teeth and looked me over.

Disgust wriggled through my stomach.

"We'll need to investigate the scene," Officer Randall said.

"Of course. It's—" I turned to point.

We all froze as a man ran out of the trail's entrance.

I noticed his wild eyes first, then his hair, pushed in all directions like he'd been tugging at it. He wore black cargo pants and a black hoodie. The knees of his pants were smudged with dirt, as well as around his ankles, above his dusty hiking shoes. He saw us and let out a shriek before jolting to a stop. He jerked to the right, paused and jerked left, then froze again.

I looked from the man to the cops to Hennie, who returned my expression of shock. I thought back to her saying, "What if the murderer shows up?" Surely, if this man had just killed someone, he wouldn't have stuck around the scene. Would he? Fear shot through my insides, and I turned to the police.

They didn't seem to know what to do. Officer Longshore jerked his head subtly as if telling Randall to handle it, but Officer Randall shook his head.

Finally, Officer Longshore took a step forward and addressed the panicked man. "We'll need to ask you a few questions, if you could stay right here, please."

"Uhh... I..." The man's frantic gaze jumped from person to person. "I didn't do it!" He held up his hands and grew pale. Then he turned around and around in circles, searching the ground as he patted himself down. "My phone! I can't find my phone!"

Officers Longshore and Randall approached the man and questioned him as another police cruiser pulled up. Two more officers joined the group talking to the man, who still appeared hysterical from what I could see. The new officers continued talking to him as Longshore and Randall walked away to approach Hennie and me.

"We'll need you to take us to the scene," Longshore said.

I gulped and nodded. "Do we know where exactly...?"

Randall looked down at a notepad. "Our witness, Isaac"—he gestured toward the frantic man—"claimed it was a place called Ribbit Rock Overlook."

The north trail ran along the top of Ribbit Rock. The drop from the trail to the bottom of the tall cliff face had to be eighty feet at least. Enough to kill someone, especially since they would be landing on rocks. That confirmed it was an accident, didn't it? The hiker got too close to the edge and slipped over.

"It's at least a mile in," I told them, eyeing Randall's middle dubiously.

"Lead the way," Longshore said.

I headed down the north trail and Hennie caught up to me in a few steps. I shot her a look. "I know where the overlook is."

"Figured you could use some protecting."

I glanced over my shoulder to the two officers following me.

Hennie looked back, too, then leaned closer. "I don't trust the two of them to do much if something goes down."

We walked for several minutes, the gravel crunching under our feet. The walk felt incredibly long and we were maybe halfway there.

Hennie snatched a long stick from beside the trail and used it to walk with. "Guess this isn't going to be too good for business, huh?"

"Bad press can be good press. Hopefully, the attention will bring new bookings."

"If they catch the murderer fast, it might."

"It's not a murder. At Ribbit Rock? Has to be an accident. When I was a kid, a man slipped while repelling down it and got hurt. Horrible arm break, but I guess he was lucky."

I tried to think back to any legal ramifications from that event, but I'd been much too young at the time. There were no railings of any sort that I could recall. Nothing to warn hikers of the danger. My chest tightened.

Hennie shook her head. "Hate to tell you, but our little friend in black looked damn guilty to me, running out of the trail the way he did."

"It's not murder." I pressed my teeth harder into my gum, wishing I had ice instead. The little knot in my neck that I'd worked so hard to get out—months with my chiropractor in the city—burned and demanded attention. My fingers found it easily and worked at it.

When we neared the rock formation, I slowed my pace. I didn't want to be the first to see the body. I told the officers, "It's just around the bend."

They went ahead with notebooks in hand. I was content to turn back and leave them to their work, but Hennie grabbed my sleeve.

"Don't you want to see the crime scene?"

I growled in frustration. "It's not—"

"Hush. I know you're a big city law partner from the stories your grandma told. Face the truth, honey. You need to know what you're dealing with, here. Get your head outta the sand."

I wanted to argue, but her logic was sound. "You're right." Whether it turned out to be an accident or not, I needed to see for myself what the situation was.

We approached the overlook, where the officers were taking photos and making notes. I took a moment to study the scene, trying to see any place a liability might hide. As I suspected, there was no railing. A sign told hikers it was the Ribbit Rock Overlook but with no indication of the possible danger. Not good.

Near the edge of the overlook, the ground seemed to be disturbed. Perhaps feet shuffling in the dirt? Hands grabbing at the ledge? A food wrapper lay nearby. Cheese curls, opened, with a few pieces still inside the small bag. Some distance away, a phone in the dirt. Could that be Isaac's missing phone?

I inched closer, keeping a careful distance from the police. When they weren't looking, I snuck my phone from my pocket and took photos. I ventured close enough to the edge to see the bright purple pants and had to pull back. I almost knocked Hennie over in my haste to get away.

"You okay?" she asked.

My stomach turned. I put my hand over my mouth and shook my head. The woman who had come into the office earlier looking for a cold drink. The one who had annoyed me. The one who I had annoyed in my lack of purchase options. She now lay dead at the bottom of the cliff. And it might be at least partially my fault due to negligence.

Hennie put her hand on my shoulder. "I'll take some photos of the body."

I nodded and faced the trail until she returned to my side a few minutes later.

"I got some good ones," she said, flicking through photos on her phone. "Want to see?"

I shook my head.

"Shh, here they come." She tucked her phone quickly in her pocket and put on a smile for Officer Longshore.

"Thank you, ladies," he said. "We've got some important things to do here, so you can head on back."

My feet took off, never so eager to walk a mile as in that moment. Hennie matched my fast pace. Neither of us spoke. When we exited the trail, I headed straight to the office while Hennie walked to the wildlife area.

Inside, a man stood facing the front counter, arms at his sides, wearing khaki pants and a polo shirt. His broad back and stiff demeanor screamed cop.

"They're at the north trail," I told him.

He turned to face me. I sucked in a breath and tried not to react, but my heart skipped a beat. Sweat broke out on my neck. His combination of tanned skin and dark hair with beard was extremely attractive, but his serious gaze and muscular build also made him intimidating. A wave of fear shivered behind the thrill that ran through me.

"I'm sorry?" he asked.

"The other cops." I pointed in the general direction. "They're by the north trail entrance. Two of them are at the scene."

He pulled his eyebrows together. "I'm not a cop. I'm here about the handyman job."

"How did you know about that? The ad didn't even run yet."

"My aunt works at the paper."

"Oh." I had no idea what I should do next with a prospective employee. My plan had been to research and worry about the hiring process later, but later had come sooner. "Do you... have a resume?"

"For a handyman job?"

The phone rang and I reached over to grab it, grateful for a distraction.

"Thank you for calling Cedar Fish Campground. This is Thea. How can I help you?"

The woman on the other end of the line said, "Hello, I have a site booked for August? And well, I've heard about what's going on over there, and I was just wondering what sort of security you all have to make sure nothing like this happens again. I don't know if I want to bring my kids to a campground where they could be murdered."

My mind whirled and took a moment to click into action. "I understand your concern, but... I'm sorry, who told you that?"

"It's all over town."

"I don't see how it can be." I chuckled nervously. "The cops haven't even left the scene yet. It looks like an accident to me."

"Uh huh. So, what I'm hearing is, you have no security, is that correct?"

"Well, we have video cameras and... police are... nearby."

She let out a long sigh. "I think I'm going to have to just cancel. I'm sorry. I can't take the chance that my family will be murdered in their sleep."

"Well, I can assure you that—"

"Can you, though? Can you assure me they'll be safe?"

"Well, as safe as—"

"That's what I thought."

She hung up with a click. Great. Somehow the word was out before the police even determined that a crime had taken place. I rubbed at the spot on my neck.

My prospective employee looked relaxed, his dark eyes in no hurry to do much of anything but observe me. I ignored the excitement I felt as my gaze slid over his rugged face and body.

"I'm sorry," I said. "I don't even know if I can afford to hire someone. At this rate, I'll need a security guard before a handyman."

He narrowed his eyes slightly. "When you walked in here, you thought I was a cop. Why?"

I shrugged. "You just looked like one."

He pulled his mouth into a sideways smirk. "I was a cop. For twelve years. And a marine for two years after that. I can do security and fix things."

I opened my mouth to object, but it made sense. I could say I had a full-time security guard on staff, and that might ease the concerns of any of my patrons. Unlike Curtis, this man appeared plenty strong and capable of doing any gruff work.

"I don't think I can afford to pay much," I admitted.

"Maybe we can work out a deal. You have sites with full hooks ups for campers?"

"Yes."

"I would consider it a portion of my compensation if I could pick one and set up a permanent site."

A 24-hour security guard on the premises? Someone who could fix a broken pipe in the middle of the night? That should have always been a live-in position.

"Sounds like a fabulous deal, so long as you agree to be on call pretty much all of the time."

He nodded. "So long as you understand that on occasion, in his time off, a man likes to have a few beers and may be unable to perform certain duties on short notice." He pulled his mouth into a charming half smile. "I'm out here to enjoy life and make the most of it. I'm a hard worker, but I do intend to play hard, too."

I swallowed the knot in my throat. "My Grandad Fish always said that a person should only play as hard as he works. That's why he worked so hard—he liked to play hard, too."

"Sounds like a fine man."

"He was." I blew out a breath. "I can use help right away, so when can you start?"

"I don't have any plans for today."

"Great. Because my to-do list grows by the hour." I dug around in the file cabinets behind the counter, hoping for some kind of employment application. "I'm sorry. I'm a little unprepared. I didn't expect anyone to come so soon. Oh." I paused and looked at him. "Any chance your aunt can cancel my ad and save me a few bucks?"

He chuckled. "I'll see what I can do."

"I'll have to find our employment applications and have you fill one out. Legal reasons and for payroll."

"Sure."

I stuck my hand out to him. "Thea Pagoni, by the way. Owner."

He shook my hand. "Pleased to meet you. Nolan Cade."

"Pleased to meet you back. So, you used to be a cop..."

CHAPTER 4

When I'd finished explaining the situation to Nolan, we walked outside and over to the trail's entrance, where the police were still milling around. I showed Nolan the photos I'd snuck and the ones Hennie had taken and sent me.

"They'll confiscate your phone if they know you have those," Nolan warned. "But that's helpful. Smart."

"I was a lawyer for ten years."

His eyes widened. "You're not related to the Pagoni of Stevenson and Pagoni, are you?"

"I'm the Pagoni. Or was."

"Partner." He whistled. "Impressive. And you left to come out here and run a campground?"

I lifted one shoulder. "Needed a change."

"I hear that."

"But it looks like this accident or murder or whatever it is might mess everything up."

"I think your chances of this being an accident are slim."

My heart sunk. "Why do you say that?"

"The police aren't treating it like an accident."

"But. Isn't that a standard thing? To treat every scene like a crime scene until they know for sure?"

"Oh, they're treating it like a crime scene. Because it is one."

"I told you." Hennie walked around the corner of the large pavilion, shotgun still in hand. "We need some security around here."

"I just hired some." I held my hand out toward Nolan. "Meet Cedar Fish's new security guard/handyman."

They shook hands and exchanged names.

"Why are you both so convinced it was murder?" I asked.

"The way that hoodlum, Isaac, came running out of the trail," Hennie said. "And wearing all black like he was up to sneaking."

"The crime scene showed signs of foul play," Nolan added.

"Such as?" I opened the photo again to look at it, but quickly looked away. The photo was easier to see than the real scene, but I could only pretend it was fake for so long before my mind replayed that woman walking into the store, looking for a cold drink.

Curtis shuffled away from the shed near the wildlife enclosure.

Nolan moved closer to me and pointed to the photo as he spoke. "Signs of a possible struggle in the dirt here. Some of the grass has been kicked up." He slid to the photo of the body. "The dirt on top of the body could be a sign of someone else being at the scene."

"Or that could have happened as she fell," I said.

"It could have," he agreed. "But, as Hennie pointed out, there is also the suspicious person of interest."

"You think Isaac did it?" I asked.

"He's likely a suspect," Nolan said. "What about these cameras?" He pointed to one hanging from the roof of the pavilion.

"They don't work," I said.

"Sure they do." I hadn't seen Curtis sneak closer, but he had finished his task of feeding the goats and was inching toward us.

"I don't know about that," I said.

The pavilion camera featured a foot-long tail of a wire that ended in a fray.

"I think some of them work," Hennie said. "I've seen something playing on the monitor in the office."

I shrugged. "Then let's go check."

The four of us entered the office and looked at the blank camera monitor. Curtis reached out to turn it on. The screen was divided into nine boxes. Eight of them were black. The one that displayed a low-quality image didn't show much of value.

"A bird's nest?" I stared at the round nest that filled the frame and the little mama whip-poor-will tending to her babies.

"Works," Curtis said, and eased onto his stool.

I turned to Nolan. "Do you think you can adjust the camera to show some of the campground?"

He nodded.

"I'll add it to the list." I put the camera's tape from today into the safe in my office, just in case, then retrieved my notebook and spread it open on the front counter. "This is everything so far," I told Nolan.

He looked my list over, nodding slowly as he did. "Where should I start?"

I blew out a breath. "I guess with the things that pose a danger? Like the burned-out bulbs and broken window in the rec hall. Maybe it'd be better if I gave you a tour of the grounds. We can discuss things as we go."

Nolan headed out the door and Hennie winked at me. "Have a nice tour."

She and Curtis waved as I left the office to catch up to Nolan.

* * *

I woke up early the next morning and couldn't fall back asleep. Eventually, I gave up the fight with my active brain and got dressed. Today would call for just a little makeup. Enough to cover the dark circles under my eyes so I didn't look so zombified.

I had managed to get some unpacking done yesterday evening after a long day of working on the campground and trying not to obsess over the murder. Thanks to my drastic downsizing before leaving St. Louis, I didn't have much. It had been easier to sell the furniture and other household goods I wouldn't need at my grandparents' fully furnished cabin. My vast wardrobe of business attire was unusable to me now, as was my sizable collection of law books. It was better to have a nice, clean slate. I didn't want anything in my new life that reminded me of Russell, our house, or our life together. Except for Archer. I sorely missed my spunky little terrier, and the absence of a pet made the place feel colder than it should.

I popped fresh ice cubes from the freezer tray into a travel mug and headed out the door toward the north trail. The police had finished up in the evening and had taken down the crime-scene tape after clearing the scene of evidence and the body, but I didn't feel right about letting people on the trail until I knew what the scene looked like now.

I crossed between the pool and playground and saw Dill walking toward the office. I called to her. She happily changed directions to come to me and rub against my legs as I bent to pet her. She had never lived full-time indoors, but on occasion, my sister and I had been allowed to have

Dill sleep between our sleeping bags. Maybe I could convince her to sleep in the cabin at night to keep me company.

I continued on my way, walking the first mile of the north trail at a quick pace. I slowed as I neared Ribbit Rock Overlook. I knew the body and evidence were long gone, but I still hesitated. The overlook held a creepy presence for me now, as if the ghost of the victim lurked nearby, watching. I couldn't help imagining falling or being pushed over the edge and landing on the rocks. I shivered the image away and forced myself to be observant.

I dared to peek over the edge, wary of slipping myself. Of course, there was nothing but rocks below. Nothing to indicate what had taken place just a day ago. I had no idea how the coroner had managed to retrieve the body. Nolan mentioned a rope and much difficulty, but I hadn't wanted details. I'd been glad to let him oversee that event and help any way he saw fit.

As I turned back, satisfied that the trail appeared normal, my gaze fell on a glint of white under a bush. Closer inspection revealed a photograph. Judging from the size and square shape, it was likely from a newer Polaroid camera. I didn't touch it—maybe it had fingerprint evidence—but I took a photo of it. The photo showed a blurry background—most likely the view from that spot—and a smudge of red that looked to me like an arm moving.

If the photo was still there, maybe the cops hadn't seen it. I hurried back down the trail and into the office.

As I'd been directed to, I dialed the direct line to Officer Longshore.

"I think I found some missed evidence," I told him after reminding him who I was.

"Missed evidence? I highly doubt that."

"Well, I saw a photograph at the scene, stuck under a bush. It would have been easy to miss."

He grunted his disbelief. "I'll have someone come take a look. You didn't touch it, did you?"

"Of course not."

"Good girl."

I bristled at the term. Before I could say something, Nolan walked in, and I found myself distracted.

"Make sure no one disturbs it, and we'll be down soon," Longshore said.

"Okay, thanks." I hung up.

"Morning, Thea," Nolan said.

"How was your first night? You get all set up?"

"Yup. Peaceful and quiet."

"Good. Look what I found." I showed him the photo of the photo. "Do you think it could be the killer?"

"Are we calling it a murder now?"

"No. But just in case."

He chuckled. "Could be anything."

"What could be?" Hennie burst through the doors, fresh mud falling from her boots. "What'd I miss?"

Irritation spiked in my chest. I glared at the chunks of mud on the office floor, but she seemed oblivious. I had no idea why she was even there. I reached for my cup and chomped a piece of ice.

"Back again?" I asked.

"Well, we have a crime to solve, don't we?" She stomped over to us and looked over Nolan's shoulder at the photo.

I thought about sending her away but having extra help couldn't hurt. And I had to admit, though I found her annoying at times, it was nice to feel like I might have a new friend. Maybe she was lonely, too. My grandma had told me once that Hennie lived alone since her husband passed many years ago. Anyone who had been friends with my grandparents automatically gained points in my book. I decided to put my own issues aside and let her in on the update.

"I found a photo at the scene," I told her. "But Officer Longshore didn't seem too impressed."

"Well." Nolan huffed.

"Well what?" I asked.

"I'm not too impressed with him," Nolan said. "Or any of the officers I saw on the scene."

"They're not used to dealing with this sort of thing," Hennie said. "I guess they'll call in the big guys from town to handle it."

"Maybe even some detectives and a homicide task force from the city," Nolan added.

"No way!" I said. "I can't have a bunch of detectives and city cops poking around my campground."

"Are you planning to obstruct justice?" he asked playfully.

"I am intending to prove that this was, in fact, a sad accident. That woman came into the store. I saw her. She was alone."

"That doesn't mean much," Nolan said. "She could have met someone on the trail."

"It's just not as likely as her slipping and falling over the edge."

Hennie and Nolan gave me looks that said they weren't buying it. Curtis pushed through the door and gave us head nods as he passed.

"Wait until you hear the latest," I told him.

He waved us off. "I have a puzzle to do."

"This investigation is much more interesting than a crossword puzzle, don't you think?"

"I want no part of any such thing." He scooted onto his stool and bent over a paper, glasses on and pencil in hand.

I turned back to Nolan and Hennie. "Now what?"

"Tell me where you want to start, and I'll get on it," Nolan said.

Hennie smirked and wiggled her eyebrows at me. I rolled my eyes.

"Well, do you think we can ask around to see if anyone knew the..." I gulped and forced myself to say the name of the victim the police had released to us. "If anyone knew Charlene Kirby?"

"I meant around the campground," Nolan said. "What do you want me to fix first?"

"Don't you want to solve this? Figure out at least if it was an accident or a murder?"

"Ain't no accident," Hennie said.

"Then don't you want to figure out who did it?" I asked.

"The police are investigating. I can't get involved," Nolan said.

"But you used to do this for a living!"

"Used to. Exactly."

I looked at Hennie questioningly.

"I can't help you much as far as knowing people," she said. "I keep to myself pretty well. But I can tell you someone who knows everyone. Enid Huff."

"Right," I said. "I should say hi to her anyway. Thank her again for helping me on my first night."

"I'm going to find something to fix," Nolan said.

"Actually, I was thinking. Can you check out Ribbit Rock Overlook and come up with a plan to install some kind of railing or fence? I don't want anyone else to fall over that cliff. And I want to post a sign warning people of the danger."

"That's a fine idea." He nodded and walked out.

"Let's go bug Enid," Hennie said.

"That's okay. I can go alone."

"This is the most exciting thing that's happened around these parts in a decade. You think I'm going to let you have all the fun?" Hennie trailed behind me.

I walked to my car and Hennie scoffed. "This is what you're driving around a campground? A Lexus? I guess city lawyers need to show off."

"I didn't have time to get something more practical." I wouldn't admit to her that I hadn't considered selling it, but she had a point. My car was covered in a layer of grime already, aside from the brand-new tires that had been installed yesterday afternoon. The car would be no help if I needed to haul or pull something. It would also bring a nice chunk of change, and I'd likely need every dollar I could scrape up.

I drove to Rollie's, crunching ice as we sped along. All I could think was, the faster this was solved, the faster things would go back to normal. I hadn't even had time to make a new normal before this all crashed down on me.

I turned into Rollie's parking lot. Every tiny stone that hit my car was another sign I should sell it. Luxury cars weren't made to handle campgrounds or country life.

We walked up the front steps, and Hennie stopped to pet the dog in the doorway. "Good ole Sunny Boy."

We found Enid behind the post office counter, selling stamps to a man who held a stack of envelopes. When she'd finished, she turned to us eagerly.

"Oh, my goodness, I can't believe it!" Enid waved her hands in the air. "A murder right here in our tiny part of the world. It's just terrible."

"We don't know it was a murder for sure," I insisted.

"Well, that's what everyone is calling it," Enid said.

"How did everyone find out so fast? I don't get it."

"You know the saying." Enid came out from behind the counter. "Good news travels fast. But good gossip travels faster."

"And how," Hennie added.

After we'd made sure Enid was up on the latest details, I asked, "Did you know Charlene Kirby?"

Enid put her hands on her hips. "Well, let me tell you about Charlene and her twin sister, Marlene. Those Kirby girls are always causing drama."

"How so?" I asked.

"Just last week the two of them came in here. Right in the middle of the cereal aisle, they start arguing over some guy. I thought I was going to have to break them up."

"Some guy..." I repeated. "You don't know who?"

Enid shook her head. "They didn't say any names, but one wanted the other to break up with him and the other one was jealous over something the first one did. Oh, what a mess. They scared customers away!"

"The sister would be a good person to talk to," I said. "And whoever that guy is. Jealousy can lead to rage, and that can lead people to do crazy things."

"Unless it was an accident." Hennie winked.

I sighed. "Right."

"I don't know about all that," Enid said. "But I don't think too many people are sad to see Charlene go, if you know what I mean. She was known for flying off the handle constantly. I wouldn't be surprised if she was killed."

"Who do you think is the most likely suspect?" I asked.

"Oh, I don't know," Enid said.

"Obviously, the guy Isaac Lang who was there at the scene," Hennie said. "He looked guiltier than I've ever seen a man look in my life, and he was the one who found the body. Had to be him."

"Maybe." I tapped my lips. "But a jealous sister and whatever the deal is with this guy could have something to do with it. I wonder if anyone else saw anything."

CHAPTER 5

When we returned to the campground, Curtis informed me that the police had come, had walked down the trail, and then left after being there for just a few minutes. I guessed they'd taken photos of the photo I'd found, but they must not have any questions for me about it.

I walked to the north trail and checked the logbook—the old notebook kept safe from the elements in a metal box at the trail's entrance.

"I can't believe I didn't think of this before," I told Hennie. "Do you think the police checked it?"

"If they're smart, they did. So, nope."

I took a photo of the latest page. No Charlene listed. No Isaac either. "I'm going to compare these names with our bookings."

As we walked to the office, the tang of freshly mowed grass filled my nose. The front of the campground already looked much better.

Inside the office, I found Nolan leaning against the counter, talking to Curtis. Nolan had changed into shorts and a t-shirt, both of which looked dirty and sweaty.

"I see that Curtis is training you well," I told Nolan.

"Came inside to find these." He held up a box of lightbulbs. "I'm off to apprehend some burnouts."

"We found out that Charlene has a twin—Charlene and Marlene—and they like to cause drama." I went to the reservation book and checked it against the list from the trail log. Ice shot through my body when I saw the name.

"What is it?" Nolan asked.

I gulped. "Isaac Lang is staying here. He's been here since the night before the murder. And if he's the killer, that means..." I wrapped my arms around my waist.

"I've been keeping an eye on him," Nolan said.

My eyes darted to his. "You have?"

He nodded. "I happen by his campsite every so often. Everything has seemed fine. I'll let you know if it doesn't."

My shoulders released and my chest relaxed. "Thank you."

"Who else is in there?" Hennie asked.

I picked the book up again. "That group of twenty-somethings went hiking yesterday, and so did that family with the toddler. I think I saw the other family, with the two older kids, eating lunch near the trail entrance. I can talk to all of them after I talk to Isaac and Marlene."

"Uhh..." Nolan gave me a questioning look. "I don't think that's a good idea. Let the police talk to the sister and the prime suspect."

"You think Isaac Lang is the prime suspect?"

Nolan nodded. "He was the one who found the body, and he does seem shifty. And that's why you shouldn't go talk to him."

"I don't think the police even checked the log, though," I protested.

"I guess if you want to talk to the campers staying here, you're within your right," he said. "Just don't get in the way of a murder investigation."

"It could still be an accident," I said.

"Could be," he agreed sarcastically.

"I'm going to see what I can find out." I picked up my notebook.

"And I'm going to get back to the rec hall," Nolan said. "Let me know when you want to talk about ideas for a railing."

"Oh, perfect. After this." Hopefully, he'd found a cheap solution. We couldn't afford much, but we couldn't afford to do nothing, either.

Hennie waved at me as I walked out of the office and muttered something that sounded like, "Have to check on my bees," before taking off on her four-wheeler. I'd assumed she'd want to tag along to find out more. Maybe

Nolan was right if even Hennie was hesitant to go talk to possible suspects.

I stopped by my cabin to grab my pocketknife. Not that I would know how to use it to defend myself, but I felt better having something on me that could be a weapon. Even if Nolan was keeping tabs on Isaac, he couldn't watch him every second.

I approached the first campsite, where the family with the toddler was staying. The father sat by the fire, roasting hot dogs. The mother chased after the small boy. Toys littered the site, and a collection of small clothing hung haphazardly off a sagging clothing line.

"Hi there!" I called to them. "Sorry to interrupt your lunch, but I was wondering if I could ask you a few questions. I'm Thea, the owner of the campground."

"Oh sure," the mother said. "We've been having a lovely time." Her young son held a bun-less hot dog and took a large bite of it as he laughed and took off running.

"Does this have to do with all the cops we saw yesterday?" the father asked. "We wondered what was going on."

"I'm afraid there was an accident on the north trail," I said. "I saw your names on the hiking log. I wondered if you had seen or heard anything unusual."

The mother nodded, but then ushered the boy into the tent. She came back out a moment later, alone. "I heard a scream," she said quietly, while looking toward the tent. "Did someone die?"

I decided to skip the death question in hopes she'd make her own conclusion and I wouldn't have to say it. Instead, I asked, "What sort of scream?"

"I thought it was a woman," the mother said.

"Do you know about what time that was?"

"Afternoon sometime?" She gestured toward the tent with her thumb. "He usually goes down for his nap around two, so it was before that."

"I'm not convinced," the father said. "The way our son shrieks? That's probably what you heard."

"I know what our son's cries sound like," the mother snapped. "It was not him."

The boy cried out suddenly. It didn't sound to me like a woman screaming, though it was rather shrill.

The mother huffed and folded her arms. "See. That scream means he just pooped his pants." She took the hot dog stick from her husband. "Why don't you go find out if I'm right?"

Discomfort wriggled in my chest as the father stood up with an angry look on his face.

"Thank you both!" I backed quietly and quickly away as they broke into an argument and the toddler screamed again.

I headed to the next campsite, where the group of young adults was staying. The six of them wore athletic clothing and tossed a tennis ball back and forth, taking turns catching it with a Velcro mitt. Music played from a phone sitting on the picnic table. I would have guessed their site would be messy, but aside from several food wrappers sitting by the fire and some cans by the trash bag, it was fairly neat. I introduced myself and asked what they'd seen.

"Oh man, I knew something was up with that," one of the guys said. "We heard a man and woman."

"Yeah. They were arguing," one of the ladies said.

Another lady added, "I thought we should break it up."

"We just didn't want to get involved," one of the guys said.

"Did you hear anything specific that was said?" I asked.

They took a moment to think.

One of the ladies confessed, "It was something like, 'Are you out of your damn mind?' and it was the female who said it." Her words took on an accusatory tone, but she shrugged and tossed the ball.

The ball bounced on the ground and one of the guys dove for it. He landed in the dirt and the rest of the group burst into laughter and cheers as he caught it before it bounced again. I held up a hand and thanked them, but it was clear they'd already moved on and forgotten about my questions.

I found the last campsite, where the family was hanging out in camp. The two older kids collected twigs and kindling. The dad chopped a log into smaller pieces of wood while the mom prepared food at the picnic table.

I approached the mom and introduced myself, still careful to call it an "accident," though it was getting harder to deny a murder as details of the event came out.

"We were there for a few hours," the mom explained. "We had lunch and took advantage of your cornhole boards. I know that we saw a family with a young boy because he said hello. There was a group of grown-up kids—being kind of loud if you ask me. And I think a couple."

"What did the couple look like?" I held my pen ready to write down all the details she could give me.

"We didn't really see them. They were entering the trail as we were setting up lunch. I just saw two people walking away. One had on these awful purple pants." She shook her head. "Why do these young girls think leggings are pants? They're not."

I gave her a smile of agreement, but I'd been hoping for more. "So, you don't know who the woman in purple was with?"

"No. Sorry."

At least she had confirmed the groups I thought were hiking that day. And even if she hadn't seen the couple, she'd seen *a* couple, and that was most likely Isaac and Charlene, like I'd suspected.

"Thank you so much." I headed back to the office, eager to share my latest updates.

As I walked, Hennie on her four-wheeler came zipping out of the woods, down an unmarked trail to the west that I guessed led to her cabin. She must have an uncanny sense for knowing when I had something to spill.

"How are those bees doing?" I called to her.

"Busy buzzing!" She called back as she passed me and parked her four-wheeler near the office.

I'd have to get used to Hennie being around all the time, whether I liked it or not. We entered the store, then my office. I spread my notebook open on the desk.

"You talk to the suspects?" she asked.

"Witnesses, and yes. Someone saw a couple, so I'm thinking that had to be Isaac and Charlene, right?"

"Well, we know they both had to be on the trail at some point."

"But this makes it seem like they were together," I said. "Do you think the police know that?"

"Hard to say."

"I'll have to ask Nolan."

Hennie made a little sound and gave me a strange smile.

"What's that for?" I asked.

"That Nolan is one fine-looking man."

I lifted a shoulder. "Sure. He's also my employee."

"And it seems that you're both single..."

"I'm not looking for anything," I said.

"Maybe not, but I think you found it."

I shook my head. "I can't date an employee. And I just got out of a divorce. Six years down the drain."

"Six years. Any kids?"

The ache barely flared any longer. I pushed it aside, as always. "No kids. At first it was all about our careers, and

then when we tried, it just didn't happen. We had a dog—
Archer. A terrier. He was like our kid."

"I haven't seen a dog around."

"No, and you won't." I couldn't hold the bitterness back
from my voice. "I lost him in the divorce."

"Don't you get some kind of visitation rights?"

"Not for dogs."

"You'd think being a lawyer that you'd get a better deal
than that."

"Yeah. You'd think." My jaw clenched and I reached for
my travel mug. Just one small piece of ice swam in a puddle of water. I chomped it hard. "The law failed me. And
that's part of the reason I gave up on it."

Hennie slumped in her chair and put her elbows on the
desk. "That's about the saddest thing I ever heard. I wondered what in the world could make a big city law partner
give it all up and come to run a broken-down campground."

"All those years together and it turns out, I didn't know
him at all. He turned on me and then took everything. It's
weird how having so much taken away makes you want to
give up everything else."

"I know it." She nodded sadly. "When I lost my Charles,
nothing mattered for a long while. I have to say, it was
partly your grandmother that got me back on track. She
believed in me. She helped me start Hennie's Honey. She
was my first customer, and she vowed to order from me
every week. And she did. Well, that is, until this week."

I dropped my head as the guilt tightened my throat. "I'm sorry. I didn't know any of that. I just got here and saw how much needed to be done and..."

Hennie reached over to swing her arm over my shoulder. "It's alright. You'll learn our ways around here. You're one of us, even if you've been gone a while. Cedar Fish is in your bones."

"I can feel it." I took a deep breath and closed my eyes. "I feel more relaxed here. Even with all that's gone on, I'm glad I came. It beats city traffic any day."

"Couldn't pay me to live there."

I tapped my pen on my notebook. "And that's why we have to figure this out. An unsolved murder could shut us down. I need this to work. I need this fresh start."

"Then, let's get to it."

CHAPTER 6

I heard her before I saw her, which was fast becoming the norm with Enid. "Hel-looo there campers!" She scuttled through the rec hall door in a knee-length magenta cardigan covered in crocheted flowers, struggling with a Crockpot. The door banged hard behind her.

"Hey there. How's it going?" I said. Then to Nolan, who sat across the picnic table from me, "Let's add that door to the list. See if you can get it to close more quietly."

I jotted it down while Nolan took the Crockpot from Enid and set it on the table.

The scent ignited a livid hunger in my stomach. Rich beef and tomato with so much garlic and onion I could taste the smell of it. The day had slipped into evening, and I couldn't recall eating anything since that morning.

Enid explained, "This recipe makes far too much for just little old me, and it's too hard to halve."

When I looked at Nolan, his eyes were round and wild with desire. We both gulped and our gazes met. I wondered if he was thinking what I was thinking: *How fast can we get rid of Enid so we can eat?*

"I thought maybe it'd been a while since the two of you had seen a home-cooked meal." Enid gave us a mothering look of reproach and produced two plastic forks from her cardigan pocket. "You eat. I just wanted to give you the latest, and then I'll be on my way. It's almost my bedtime."

I glanced at my smart watch. 8:15. She must be an early bird. "It smells amazing," I said. "Did you eat already?" I pushed aside my to-do notebook.

"Hours ago. Go on, now. It's my grandmother's keftedakia."

Though Enid supplied forks, there were no bowls or plates in immediate reach, so I lifted the lid off the Crockpot and stabbed one of the small meatballs smothered in red sauce. I stuck the first forkful in my mouth and closed my eyes as the flavors melted over my tongue.

Enid went on. "So, I wanted to tell you that I remembered something. That Charlene was in my store on Monday—the same day she died. And, do you know what she bought?"

I swallowed and blinked at her. "A cold drink?"

"No. She bought cheese curls."

"The same brand found at the scene?" I dug in for another forkful. Nolan hadn't stopped while I paused to talk and was now ahead of me by several bites.

"Of course," Enid said. "And do you know how badly those things stain? I can't stand them, leaving orange all over my fingers. I wondered if that could be a clue."

Nolan spoke with a full mouth, which I couldn't blame him for. "Charlene's fingers had some orange smears."

I nearly choked. "What! You saw cheese stains and didn't say anything? How could you leave out something so important?" I snatched my phone from the table and scrolled to the photo, then stuck another meatball in my mouth and chewed while inspecting the image again.

Nolan shrugged. "All it means is that she was the one who ate the cheese curls."

When I thought it through, he was right. She must have been eating the cheese curls just before going over the cliff. But that didn't point to anyone else being involved.

"It doesn't help us solve it?" Enid asked.

I gave an apologetic smile. "Guess not. But it's good to know." My stomach finally felt full, but I stuffed in another two keftedakia anyway. "I did talk to some of my campers and they heard a woman scream and a couple arguing."

"Now, that's something," Enid said hopefully.

"Could be." I set my fork down. "Those meatballs were amazing, Enid. Thank you for bringing them over."

"Oh, it's nothing. They're so easy. Just beef, onion, egg, and spices."

"I'll have to try it sometime," I said.

"Let me know if you need someone to test the recipe," Nolan added. "You know, to make sure they taste like the original. Since I'm the only other person who's tasted them."

I held back my laughter. But then an image flashed into my mind of me serving Nolan dinner in my cabin. I sucked in a breath and replaced the lid on the empty Crockpot. "I'll wash this and bring it back to you."

"Bring it back full of gossip, you hear?" Enid pointed at me before walking off.

Nolan sat back and put his hand on his extended stomach. "Good snack. What's for dinner?"

*   *   *

All night, I thought about the death. I had started to treat it more like a murder, but I still didn't like to think the word. It kept me up too late and woke me up too early. When I finally crawled out of bed, I made extra coffee and filled three travel mugs: two with coffee and one with ice.

I had come to one decision in the midst of my sheep counting. I would talk to Marlene and Isaac. Even if Nolan didn't think it was the best idea. We hadn't heard a word from the police, and the gossip around town was all based on hearsay and imagined evidence. Nothing substantial had come out. No arrests had been made. The death hadn't even been officially ruled a homicide. And all of that meant two things. One, I couldn't get in the way of the murder investigation if they hadn't declared there was one. Two, the cops didn't seem to be doing such a hot job at figuring things out.

Beyond the distressing reality of knowing someone died in my campground—though my common sense reminded me that probably other people had died there, too, over the years—I hated thinking this might be the thing that put Cedar Fish out of business. But the reservation book didn't lie.

When I envisioned closing up the office for the last time, it tore such a hole through my insides that tears burned my eyes. I couldn't let everything my grandparents built crumble. I couldn't face a second monumental failure—not so very soon after the first. I had come to heal, not to stress over murder suspects and how to convince people that the campground was safe.

I spent the early hours of the morning in my office, doing paperwork. I emailed the estate lawyer again to get an update on the status. Not much could be fixed up using our operating budget. The date crept nearer to Memorial Day weekend and it looked like the campground wouldn't be close to ready.

I decided to call the police before going any further in my own investigation. Maybe they'd made progress and I could go on with other things.

"Hello, Officer Randall," I said. "Thea Pagoni. I wanted to talk to you about the investigation."

"I've told you, I can't give you any details—"

"I have details to give you."

He blew out a breath. "Okay. What do you know?"

"I didn't know if you looked at the trail logbook, but I talked to the people who had been hiking that day, and it looks like Charlene and Isaac were probably on the trail together. Someone saw a couple, then another group heard a couple arguing, and someone else heard a woman scream. I didn't know if you knew all of that..."

"You questioned witnesses?" His tone was sharp enough to make me gulp.

"I talked with my patrons, yes. I needed to make sure, as the campground owner, that they're not distraught in any way." That sounded feasible, right?

"Leave the questioning up to the police, miss."

"So, you already knew all of what I just told you?" I demanded.

A long pause and then, "We thank you for your update, and if you should hear anything else, please let us know."

I opened my mouth to respond but heard a click before the line went dead. I set my phone down.

For a moment, I considered what Nolan and Randall told me to do. It wasn't illegal to have a conversation with someone—that much I could be sure of, since I wasn't tied to the case as a lawyer. If these people willingly talked to me, it was nothing more than gossip amongst friends. Reporters did it all the time. Police would have to prove that my questioning had caused some problem. As long as I was helping, I couldn't be hindering, could I? If I was careful, I could make sure I did nothing that was technically illegal.

I finished off my second coffee and popped a fresh ice cube in my mouth. I waved to Curtis, who sat hunched on his stool, snoring. Outside, Nolan measured the broken window in the rec hall. I slid into my car before he could stop me.

I drove to Rollie's first. With Enid's clean Crockpot in hand, I stepped over Sunny Boy, but nearly tripped over the giant, diaper-wearing turtle inching his way across the store.

"You hooo!" Enid called to me.

I turned until I saw her down one of the aisles, placing boxes of pancake mix on the shelf.

"That was fast," she said.

"I'm on a mission. Do you know where Marlene lives?"

Enid smiled with a glint in her eyes as she set the last box in place. "Why, yes I do."

I carried the Crockpot into the backroom for her and waited while she pulled a thick phonebook from under the front counter.

"I didn't think they printed those anymore," I said.

"They don't. I keep this one around."

The date on the cover was more than a decade old. "Uhh..."

"Here it is!" She pointed to an address written in small type. The listing wasn't for anyone named Marlene or Charlene, or with the last name Kirby. "Greta comes in all the time, complaining about her noisy neighbors, the

Kirby twins. She lives right next to them. This is Greta's address."

I took a photo of the listing.

"You be sure and tell me what you find out," Enid said as she closed the book and returned it to the shelf.

"I will. Thanks!"

I left Rollie's and drove to the small house that matched the address. Greta had two neighbors. One was close and the other was farther away, with a row of trees between the houses. I guessed that if a neighbor was going to bother her, it'd be the closer of the two.

I stood on the porch of what I hoped was Marlene's house for a moment, mentally reviewing my questions before I knocked.

A woman in an ill-fitting black dress yanked the door open. "Oh. Who are you?"

Her gruff voice shocked me at first, but her face was familiar. I recovered and stuck out my hand. "Thea Pagoni. Are you Marlene Kirby?"

"Yeah?" She put a limp hand in mine and made the gesture of shaking.

"I own the campground where your sister died, and I just wanted to stop by and see how you were doing."

Marlene put her hand on her hip. "Well, how should I be doing?"

"I... don't know. Not too good, I'd guess."

"Not good at all! I got this funeral today. Worst day for it, too. Who got time for all this? Not me." She made a duck face and wagged her head.

Her irritation stunned me enough that I made a mental note. No sign of sadness for a dead twin sister on the day of her funeral?

"Sorry to interrupt you on such a day," I said. "I didn't know the funeral was today. Do you have a boyfriend or anyone to... uhh... comfort you? Did Charlene have a boyfriend?"

Marlene raised an eyebrow sharply and her lip pulled up. "What have you heard?"

My eyes widened. "Nothing, just that someone in Rollie's heard you two arguing over a guy."

"Well, we're always arguing over Preston Bean. What else is new?"

"Preston? Is that Charlene's boyfriend?"

Marlene rolled her eyes. "Yeah."

"Do you think she was with him the day she died?"

"I'm sure. Bastard probably even took her to the overlook. Why?"

"Do you think Preston could have killed Charlene?"

"I wouldn't be that lucky, would I?" she barked.

Lucky? I thought back to her earlier defensiveness. Maybe Marlene was guiltier than I had thought. "Who do you think killed her?"

"Who knows. Probably that stalker, Isaac. He's not right. But that's for the police to worry about."

"Isaac Lang?"

Someone shouted from inside the house and Marlene hollered back, "I'm coming!"

"He was stalking her?" I asked. "What do you mean, 'he's not right'? What sorts of things did he do? For how long?"

"I gotta go." Marlene didn't offer so much as a wave as she shut the door in my face.

CHAPTER 7

I walked out to my car but sat there, in front of Marlene's house. In my notebook, I changed her to a suspect and added Preston Bean to my list of persons of interest. I made a note by Isaac's name. If he was stalking Charlene, there could be motive there.

I returned to the campground and walked the long loop of Walleye Circle toward Isaac's campsite. When I rounded the corner, I saw Nolan driving away slowly in his black pickup. He had mentioned that he was keeping an eye on Isaac. He must be doing regular patrols.

I slowed my walk and waited for the truck to be out of sight before approaching. A car sat parked beside the tent, but I didn't see anyone. Then I took notice of the campsite. Not a single piece of trash littered the ground. One trash bag hung from a tree, knotted neatly. The fire ring contained only charred chunks of wood. The picnic table looked scrubbed clean—cleaner than I would have believed it could look. Even the ground itself appeared to have been swept free of leaves, sticks, and other outdoor debris. Could he be so paranoid about leaving evidence behind that he'd gone overboard cleaning things up?

"Hello there? Isaac?" I called out.

The tent unzipped enough for his head to pop out. "Yeah? What?" He looked around but didn't move from the tent.

"Could I talk to you for a few minutes?"

He blinked nervously and slowly unzipped the tent door to step out. His eyes darted around and he didn't stand still. His hands looked red and chaffed. From scrubbing them too hard?

"I'm Thea, the owner of the campground, I'm trying to get some information on Charlene Kirby, to know more about who she was. Her sister mentioned that you and Charlene had a relationship. I thought you could maybe help me to... honor her memory by telling me more about her."

He huffed. "I barely knew her."

"You barely knew Charlene Kirby?"

He nodded his head hard and for too long.

"Marlene says you did know her. Well, she actually used the word 'stalker.'"

Isaac's eyes darkened and his head dropped. "I'm not a stalker."

"But you did know her. Why do you think Marlene would say that?"

Isaac lifted one shoulder. "I was interested in Charlene, but she wasn't interested back. Does that mean I'm a stalker for trying to win her over?"

"Not necessarily. Depends on what you did to try to win her over, I suppose."

"I was being romantic! I thought girls liked secret admirers!" He reached up and tugged at his hair until it stood in multiple directions. Then, as if realizing what he'd done, immediately smoothed it back down and made it neat again. He straightened his shirt and ran his hands down his pant legs.

"In what ways did you admire her? Are we talking trespassing?"

"No," he muttered. "Just like, texts and notes and stuff."

"Were you with Charlene the day she died? We all know you were both on the trail at the same time."

"I already told the cops this. I was on the trail, yeah. But I was *not* with her."

"Did you see her?"

"No. Not... not until..." He let out a strangled cry of frustration. "I was trying to do something for her!" He kicked his toe in the dirt and refused to make eye contact. When his little fit was over, he smoothed the dirt back into place with his shoe.

"What were you trying to do?"

He muttered something I couldn't understand.

"What's that?" I asked.

"I wanted her to know I loved her. I was going to spell it all out in sticks so she would see it."

"And did you?"

"Didn't have a chance," he grumbled.

"Why, what happened?"

"I got to the spot where I was gonna do it, but then my flashlight was gone. I had to go back and get it because it's my favorite flashlight. I don't go anywhere without it. But that's when I saw Charlene and—" His voice broke and he swiped his eyes. The rest came out in a rush. "I called the office but dropped my phone because I was freaking out. But I swear, I didn't see her the whole time! Well, not alive at least."

So, the phone at the scene had been his. I took quick notes and asked, "Who could have hurt her?"

His face hardened. "That jerk, Preston. I saw him on the trail, you know. The cops didn't believe me, but I saw him! He was walking alone! I mean, what more do you need to prove the guy did it?"

I raised my eyebrows. No one had seen Preston in the campground that day. But a guilty man would surely try to point the blame to someone else. "Do you know where I can find Preston?"

"I'd guess at the funeral. Paper said it's in an hour."

I checked my watch. "Thanks for talking to me." I started to walk away, but added, "I hope you're enjoying your stay at Cedar Fish Campground!"

Isaac gave a blank stare in response. Then he retrieved a broom from his tent and furiously swept the spot I had been standing in.

I hurried back to the office. Why hadn't I thought to check the paper? I used to read the *St. Louis Post-Dispatch* every day from my law office, but I hadn't considered it an important habit to keep up. If I was going to know what was going on in Outer Branson and the area around the campground, I'd have to get back to staying current on the local news.

As I entered the store, I grabbed a paper off the shelf and took it behind the counter. I almost knocked Curtis over as I passed him. He blended into the background in his brown sweater vest and sat so still on his stool, I hadn't even seen him.

"Sorry about that." I rested a hand on his shoulder to make sure he was steady.

He lifted a furry eyebrow at me. "What's that?" His book of crossword puzzles sat on top of the reservation book.

"Busy day?"

He nodded and yawned.

I searched under the front counter and found the old green address book where my grandparents kept important contact information. Our service providers were listed and so were our vendors, including Hennie's Honey.

I picked up my phone and dialed Hennie's number, then saved it before completing the call.

She answered with a loud, "Yello."

I didn't bother with small talk.

"Want to come to Charlene's funeral with me and question a possible suspect?"

"I'll be there in eight minutes."

I hung up and rushed off to my cabin to change. My usual jeans and hoodie weren't exactly funeral attire. I yanked on my black pants and a top, dug through my box of highly impractical shoes, and found one, then two of my black flats. Unfortunately, they were not matching flats, so I burrowed in deeper and eventually made a pair.

By the time I got back outside, Hennie was cruising down a path through the woods on her four-wheeler. Her flannel shirt had been replaced by an old black button-down over casual black pants. Not surprisingly, her knee-high rubber galoshes had made the cut and squished when she hopped off the four-wheeler.

"Let's do this!" She whipped a handgun from her back holster and aimed at a spot to our right. "Brought the little guy today." She tucked the gun back in. "What are we waiting for?"

I squinted at her. She probably knew how to use a gun safely and wouldn't shoot me by accident. "Nothing. Let's go."

I pulled open my car door, and we climbed in. I pretended not to see Nolan's questioning look as we turned out of the office parking lot, passing him on his way toward the front gate.

"I don't think he'd be too happy about this," I admitted.

Hennie rubbed her hands together. "No trouble. If he gives you a hard time, I have a surprise to cheer you up."

"What's that?"

"Well, it wouldn't be a surprise now if I told you, would it? You'll just have to come on back to my cabin later."

I tried not to imagine what Hennie might conjure up in her attempt to rouse my spirits. "It's too bad if he does have a problem with it. I'm the owner and he's not a cop."

"Not anymore, but whoo-eeee." She whistled. "You've got to hit that."

"Hennie!" I slapped her arm playfully. "He is my *employee.*"

"So then, fire him, nail him, and hire him back."

I covered my face with my hand.

We came to the graveyard and I parked. We quietly approached the small gathering. About ten people stood around a fresh grave. The graveyard itself wasn't big. Most headstones were small and low to the ground. Few had decorations.

We kept our distance and waited for the minister to finish. The ceremony wasn't very long or spiritual. A few Bible verses were read, but no one prayed or told stories about the deceased. Perhaps they had had a private ceremony earlier somewhere. The paper had only mentioned the burial.

When the crowd dispersed, I inspected every person in attendance. Each seemed solemn but not particularly sad or distraught. I wondered if Charlene's parents were any of the passing folks. Surely burying a child would cause anyone terrible grief.

Marlene had shown up, but I didn't see Isaac. A young man put his arm around Marlene, and she leaned her head on his shoulder. He dropped his arm quickly and walked away from her. No one else looked boyfriend age.

"I think that's him," I whispered to Hennie.

"Preston Bean?" she shouted.

His head snapped toward us and he responded with, "Yeah?"

Preston looked nothing like Isaac, who was tall and lanky. Preston had a thicker build, darker and more serious eyes, and was slightly better looking. No wonder Charlene had chosen him over Isaac.

I stepped forward. "I'm Thea Pagoni, the owner of the campground where Charlene died. I wanted to give my condolences and see how you were doing."

He shrugged and looked at the ground.

"I guess you're pretty shook up?" I offered.

"I just wish I would have been there. I could have saved her, maybe." He shrugged again and sighed.

"So, you weren't there that day?" I shifted my gaze briefly to Hennie, who raised her eyebrows back at me.

"I was working."

That meant either Isaac or Preston were lying. "Where do you work?"

He looked up at me. "A warehouse in town. Why?"

"Just… hoping you'll be able to take some time off," I said.

"Yeah," he muttered and looked down again.

Hennie nodded for me to continue.

"What do you know about Isaac Lang?"

Preston flashed a glare and looked around. "Is he here?"

"No, I saw him earlier," I said. "He… seems to think you had something to do with Charlene's death."

"He what?" Preston's jaw tightened.

"He told me he saw you on the trail that day, alone."

"He's saying I killed her?"

I lifted a shoulder and gave a half smile of agreement.

Preston's nostrils flared. "Right. After he stalked my girlfriend for months, he goes and says I killed her, trying to take the attention off himself. I'm gonna find that little—"

When he punched his fist into his palm, I jumped. Even such a little sign of violence, along with his angry tone, sent me into flight mode.

"Thank you for your time." I backed away. "Sorry for your loss."

I turned and hurried toward the parking lot.

Hennie jogged to catch up. "We need to ask him more questions!"

"Nope." I hopped into my car and started it. The moment Hennie's door shut, I pressed the gas.

"What was the point of all this if you weren't going to ask him anything else?" Hennie demanded.

"He told us enough. He had a solid alibi, so it couldn't be him, and he pointed out that Isaac is trying to shift the guilt off himself. It all makes sense."

"Okay," she said. "But you kinda rushed out of there."

"I think we made him mad, and I didn't want to stick around for that."

Hennie nodded slowly. "Fair enough. And we'll get to my surprise that much sooner!"

The dread increased in my stomach the closer we got to Hennie's cabin. I drove around the long way, since the short way was a path that nothing bigger than a four-wheeler could make.

Her cabin was nestled so deeply in the woods, it looked to be in danger of being swallowed whole. She'd decided not to tend most of the land around the cabin, opting for natural camouflage in the thick brush and trees. Beside the cabin, a few goats grazed by a barn and several chickens had free run of the grounds.

"Come around back." She gestured and I followed.

Behind the cabin sat a small, crumbling shed. The door opened with a loud shriek and a bang. Hennie bent down and pulled a blanket from the top of a metal cage. She motioned me closer. Inside the cage, a small bundle of grey and white slept on a bed of leaves.

"Aww." I preferred dogs over cats, but I certainly wouldn't turn down a kitten.

The cat stretched and stood up. I jumped back. "What is that?! That's not a cat!"

Hennie laughed. "A cat? Of course not. It's a baby raccoon, silly."

"Why do you have a baby raccoon in a cage?"

I stood back as Hennie poked a carrot at the animal. The raccoon stared at it but didn't move nearer to the food.

"He misses his mama," Hennie said. "Found him all alone and nearly dead. I gave him goat's milk in a bottle, and he loved it, but I have enough critters as it is. And you lost your dog, so it's perfect. You need each other."

I could agree I needed a pet, but somehow a raccoon hadn't exactly crossed my mind.

Hennie stood and thrust the cage at me. "I'll leave naming him up to you."

I held the cage as far away from my body as I could. "You sure it's a him?" I inspected the small animal, who now hissed at me and cowered in the corner. "I think we should let him go."

Hennie threw her hands in the air. "Are you nuts?! If you put him out in the world alone, he'll be tore up to pieces! Is that what you want?" She put her hands around her throat in a dramatic choking action.

"No, but..."

"I milked the goat extra today. Got a bunch for you right inside, and all you got to do is heat it up a little and put it in the bottle. Just like a baby."

"I don't know the first thing about babies."

Hennie waved me off. "They're easy. And taking care of a babe raccoon ain't any different."

"I'm sure there are diff—"

"I'll get you this milk, but I got things to tend to today."

And that apparently meant I'd spend the rest of the day Googling raccoons. "O... kay...?"

She banged her way out of the shed.

When I ventured out, holding the cage as carefully as I could manage, Hennie charged out of the house toward me.

"Here you are." She thrust a glass milk jug at me. "Let me know when he runs low. Every four hours should do it." She set a plastic baby bottle on top of the cage. "Call me if you need anything."

"What about your four-wheeler?"

She waved me off. "I'll walk down to get it later."

I stared after her as she went back inside the cabin. Reluctantly, I placed my new pet on the backseat of my car. Where in the world would I keep him? I didn't have a shed like Hennie did, and it still got cold at night. The day had already cooled as the afternoon faded.

I headed home and carried the cage into the living room. Having the raccoon sleep in the same room with me would be too creepy and might keep me up if he made a lot of noise.

The bottle sat beside the cage and the raccoon sniffed at it, then reached his tiny paw through the bars to touch it.

"You hungry?"

I filled the bottle with some of the milk. I thought about warming it, but that would require more effort than I could muster. I stuck the rubber nipple through the bars. He looked up at me, then decided he'd get no better delivery and sucked at the nipple.

"Guess you'll need a name." I watched him drink the milk eagerly. I tossed a few names around in my head but hadn't settled on one by the time the bottle ran empty. "Well, there, Ricky Raccoon, I gotta get back to work."

I stood in my doorway and contemplated. Something didn't seem wise above leaving a wild animal alone inside of my house. Though, taking him with me into the office didn't seem the best idea, either. I double checked the cage's latch to make sure it was secure before leaving.

CHAPTER 8

When my alarm went off for the third time, I smacked my phone with irritation. I hadn't slept well. Not that I expected to, having had to wake up every four hours to feed Ricky. But expecting hadn't made dealing any easier.

My new morning routine, which started with a warm and somewhat brown shower experience, now would include feeding the baby one last time before going off to work.

I walked down to the office building, passing the new shiny window in the rec hall. In my office, I picked up the mail that had piled up. The stack had barely shrunk by the time Nolan entered the building. Curtis looked up from his crossword and muttered a hello.

"In here," I called out.

Nolan entered and sat in the chair beside me at the table that functioned as my desk.

"That window looks nice," I said.

"Sure thing. You hear what happened last night?"

My heart leapt. "What happened?"

"Isaac was attacked."

"What! Nolan, you have to tell me these things! Why didn't you call me or come get me?"

"Hold on, now. It didn't happen here."

"Oh." My brain still worked over what an attack on Isaac could mean. "Then how did you know?"

"I have my ways."

I glared at him. "Is it a cop thing?"

"Not really. I have a scanner. I don't know why I even brought the thing since I can't sleep with it on, but it's come in handy."

"What do you know about this attack?"

"Not much," he admitted. "I heard the call go out and Isaac's name. They didn't arrest anyone. That's all I know."

"What could it mean?"

"Any number of things."

"Well, wait until you hear what I—" Oops. I forgot he wasn't supposed to know about that.

He raised an eyebrow. And waited. Then asked, "Hear about what you found out yesterday when you interviewed Marlene, Isaac, and Preston?"

"So, you know about that."

"Curtis pays a lot more attention than you think."

"Curtis?" My gaze shifted toward his hunched form.

Nolan smiled and said nothing. I rolled my eyes and spilled the details of my interviews.

"Good work," he said when I'd finished.

"You're not mad?"

"I just don't want you getting in trouble, Thea. Obstructing a murder investigation can be a serious charge."

"I don't want to get in the way, I just want to help. I don't even know if the police know about Isaac being a stalker."

"Hard to say."

"What if Isaac did it on purpose?" I said. "Got someone to beat him up to make it look like he's innocent?"

"Or Preston had himself a drink or two after the funeral and ran into the person most likely responsible for the death of his girlfriend. On top of that, he'd just been told that Isaac named him as the killer."

I bit my lip. "You think it's my fault that Isaac got beat up?"

"Not your fault. But your information might've pushed Preston over the edge."

"Is Isaac okay? Do we even know?"

"They took him to the ER, but he was in his tent a few minutes ago when I drove by."

"The ER? That sounds bad."

"Probably just standard procedure. If he's already been released, I'm sure he's fine."

I blew out a hard breath. "Can you find out who beat him up?"

He pulled his mouth into a smile that sent a flush to my cheeks. "I can try."

I spent the bulk of that day catching up on tasks that I should have been doing instead of solving a murder, like paying bills and balancing the books. I'd gone back twice to feed Ricky and play with him for a few minutes. Maybe if he was raised in a cage, he'd be tame enough to keep indoors when he got bigger.

When the time came for Ricky's next feeding, I decided to call it a night. The daylight had vanished and the insects appeared. Nolan had replaced all the burned-out bulbs, so my walk back to my cabin was well-lighted, which made me feel safer.

As I neared my front door and saw the note scribbled in marker, that safe feeling evaporated. My head jerked back and forth as I trained my eyes for signs of motion. I wanted to believe it could be a friendly note. Maybe Enid had stopped by to say hello. My gut knew it wasn't true. Though I couldn't make out the words from that distance, I could tell the writing was sharp and hard. Angry looking.

I didn't have my pocketknife or any sort of weapon. The only thing I could do was run, but part of me thought that doing that could be worse. What if whoever left the note was watching me and followed me when I ran off alone? I took my phone from my back pocket with a shaking hand.

When Nolan answered, I simply said, "I need you."

"Where are you?"

"Outside my cabin."

"Be right there."

He hung up. It wasn't two minutes before his pickup pulled in beside my car.

"What's wrong?" he asked as he hopped out.

I pointed to the note. I hadn't gone closer to it. I didn't want to touch it.

He walked up to the door and stared at the note for a minute, then yanked it off.

"What are you doing! The police might want to finger-print that!"

"They won't." He handed me the note. "Keep that. Did you go inside?"

I wrapped my arms around my waist. "No, I couldn't."

"Good. Stay here while I check it out." Nolan slid a black handgun from a holster at his back and pulled back the slide before pushing the door open with his foot.

He entered, easing along sideways until he was out of sight. I stared at the note in my hand and read the words again: "Stop asking questions or you'll end up like Charlene."

My heartbeat thumped in my ears. The last time I'd been this afraid, it hadn't turned out well.

When I looked up again, a shadow moved in the door-way. I shrieked and jumped back.

"Whoa." Nolan held up a hand. "Sorry. It's clear. Come inside."

I hurried in and right over to Ricky's cage. He stood on his back feet, sniffing around wildly. "It's okay. You're okay. We're okay." I opened the door and pulled him out, then held him close. His warmth melted into my chest soothingly as he chittered in my ear, trying to break free from my grip.

Nolan put his gun away and watched me curiously.

"So, the killer was here?"

"It's a good possibility." Nolan looked around. "Is any-thing missing? What's out of place?"

I took a brief walkthrough of the living room and kitch-en. "Everything looks fine."

"Oh."

"Why do you sound surprised?"

He glanced around again and held back a laugh. "I thought the place had been ransacked."

Boxes and their contents lay scattered across every surface.

"I've been busy and haven't had time to really unpack." I put Ricky back in his cage and walked to the kitchen. "Look what I found today though." I held up my Crockpot. One of the few kitchen items I had taken when I moved out, and I had only taken it because my mother had given it to me, and it didn't remind me of my ex.

"And what do you plan to do with that?" Nolan asked.

"Well. I planned to try Enid's meatball and sauce recipe. I have the meat prepped, I'm starving, and honestly..." I didn't know if I should admit it, but if I didn't tell him why I wanted him to stay, he might get the wrong idea. "I'm really freaked out about this, and I don't want to be alone right now. If I make you dinner, will you stay for a while?"

He looked at me for a moment before a slow smile spread across his face. "You're going to make the same keftedakia that Enid brought us the other night?"

I nodded.

"Then honey, I'll stay as long as you want."

My throat felt thick when I swallowed. "Thanks."

I got to work on the meatballs, since they would take some time to form and fry. Nolan sat on the floor, rolling a ball back and forth with Ricky as I tried to quickly put some things away.

When everything was ready, I scooped meatballs into two bowls and took a deep whiff. It smelled okay, but not the same as Enid's.

"What?" Nolan asked as I set the bowls on the large kitchen table.

"It doesn't smell right."

He took a whiff and shrugged. Then he took a bite. The surprise in his eyes faded to a hint of disgust before he put on a blank face and swallowed.

"Oh, no." I stuck my fork in and braved a bite. I almost spit it back out. The balance of spices was way off, giving it a strange bitter taste. The texture was also too crumbly. "Clearly, something is not right here."

Nolan wagged his head slowly side to side. "Oh, Lucy," he said in his best Ricky Ricardo voice.

I chuckled, but something clicked in my mind and I stopped laughing. "Wait a second."

Nolan braved another bite but had to swallow hard to get it down.

"That voice..."

"You named the raccoon Ricky and that made me think of it," Nolan explained.

"Right. No, I mean Marlene's voice. It's kinda deep and gruff. My first day here—the day that Charlene died—I listened to an old voicemail from someone, and I couldn't figure out if it was a man or woman. But Marlene has that same sort of rough voice. I think it was Marlene who called asking about the cliff."

Nolan's eyebrows shot up. "Now, that's interesting."

"Is it? Do you think that shows premeditation?"

"Possibly. She could be working with someone."

"Marlene seemed jealous, like she has a thing for Preston, maybe, and wasn't happy he chose Charlene over her. Maybe she helped Isaac kill her."

"Or helped Preston."

"Right, but if his alibi is solid, I don't think he's as likely."

Nolan nodded. "No, I'd say Isaac is still my top choice. But that sister..."

"Something's not right there. The note on my door must be from her."

"Don't assume that," Nolan warned, "but it's a possibility. Could have been anyone, really."

"We have to get those video cameras up and working again. Do you know much about that stuff?"

"I've done some basic electrical work."

"I'll do some research if you can try to assess what we have and see if any of it is usable." I grabbed my notebook and added it to my to-do list. Then I tried eating another bite but found it difficult to swallow. "Do you think there's anything I can do to make these better?"

Nolan leaned closer to his bowl and sniffed. "Add some salt?"

"I don't think that'll help it. Oh!" Something else clicked in my mind. "Some campers said they heard a man and woman arguing. But they might have mistaken Marlene's voice for a man's. Another camper said there was a couple, but that doesn't mean it was a man and a woman. Not these days. It could have been two women."

"Fair point," Nolan admitted. "We could go back and verify what they saw."

"They've all checked out of the campground." I pushed the meatballs around in my bowl, thinking. "If Marlene was jealous over Preston, maybe she pushed Charlene. It was bizarre how unaffected she seemed by her sister's death. I didn't see her crying at the funeral, either. That, to me, screams guilt."

"It would certainly be something I would've taken note of if I were investigating." Nolan got up and went to Ricky's cage.

"Murder your own twin sister? How cold does a person have to be?"

Nolan sat back down at the table, Ricky in his lap, and held his fork up to the raccoon's face. Ricky sniffed eagerly and reached for the fork. He ate the meatball and then tried to get free from Nolan's grip to get more.

"Ricky likes it." Nolan let him reach his little paw into his bowl and help himself to another meatball.

I covered my face. "I think I have a frozen pizza."

Ricky scuttled across the table and tackled my bowl next, knocking it to the floor in his haste, and causing it to shatter. Splatters of sauce flew across the floor and a meatball rolled under the chair.

"You know," Nolan said as he flicked a chunk of tomato off his shoulder, "you're going to have to move him outside before he becomes too comfortable."

"That's the point." I took a rag from the drawer and wiped at the mess. "He needs to be domesticated so he can be a good pet."

Ricky, in his new freedom and fresh energy, darted around the room, picking objects from my boxes and shaking them before throwing them down.

"Somehow," Nolan said, twisting in his chair to watch the animal at work, "I don't think that's going to happen."

CHAPTER 9

In the morning, I made coffee for Nolan and me but knew I'd need a lot more. Yesterday had been a two-mug day, but I'd had even less sleep last night. Knowing that Nolan was downstairs on the couch had helped, but not enough. Every noise had me sitting up in bed, heart racing, listening for the intruder surely breaking in. Most of the time it was only Ricky rattling the door to his cage.

When I stumbled into the living room to hand Nolan his coffee, I found him doing pushups on the floor in front of the cage. Ricky watched and chattered, cheering him on. When Nolan stopped, he flipped over and started a round of sit-ups.

"You do this every morning?" I asked.

"Got up late this morning. Usually, I get in a run and a longer workout before work."

My gym membership had been one thing I wasn't sad to leave behind when I left the city. I walked a lot. Compared to sitting in an office for eight to ten hours, that was tons of exercise. I'd gone over my step goal every day since I'd arrived.

I walked around Nolan and headed for the door. "Just lock up when you're done."

"I'm right behind you." He jumped to his feet in one fluid movement.

We walked out together, and I thought nothing of it until I heard Hennie's four-wheeler in the distance.

"Oh, no."

Nolan leaned close. "Want me to hide in the bushes?"

"No. We did nothing wrong or unethical."

A sly grin spread across his face.

"What?" I asked.

"Just thinking about the wrong and unethical option."

My face warmed. "That's... not an option." I turned on my heel and hurried past Hennie.

"Hey Thea!" she shouted to me and circled.

"Hey," I mumbled.

Hennie glanced at Nolan. He smiled and waved as he headed for his camper. Her eyes widened.

"Nolan had to come and make sure my cabin was secure because of the threatening note I got last night."

Her eyes widened even farther. "What'd it say?"

I handed it to her.

She shook her head. "That no-good son of a gun."

"Preston?" I asked.

"Him or that sister."

"That's what I thought, too."

Hennie nudged me with her elbow. "And what does, uh, Nolan say?"

"He agrees."

She wagged her eyebrows at me.

"Don't give me that look."

"When did you get that note?"

"Last night."

She burst into a goofy grin. "So, he *did* spend the night."

"On the couch. It was purely for my protection."

"That is just so romantic."

"Zero romance involved. Though he did get up to feed Ricky once for me."

"Well, there you go," Hennie said. "It's like you're married with a baby already."

"Umm... So, this note."

"Okay, okay, you're being secretive about it. I get it."

"It's really not like that," I said. "I told you, I'm not ready for a relationship."

She put a hand on my shoulder. "Honey. You can sleep with a man and not be committed to him for life, you know."

I gave her a half smile. "I'll keep that in mind. So, the note? You think it was most likely Preston?"

"Wouldn't surprise me. It's always the angry ones."

"Seems like most men have an angry streak." The engrained image of Russell's angry face flashed into my mind. I shook it off and refocused.

Hennie wagged a finger as she spoke. "You know what it is. This widespread practice of circumcision."

"The what?"

"You know, circumcising babies? It's an outrage, what they do!" She threw her hands in the air.

"It is?"

Hennie paced a few steps back and forth, becoming more animated as she continued. "All that pain, and so young? You ever have something violent done to your body against your will?" She paused to hold my gaze and a light ringing sound pulsed in my ears as she continued. "When you mess with a man like that, it messes with him for life."

My throat was like sandpaper when I swallowed. "I guess I never really thought much about it."

Hennie went on. "Well, you know how traumatic it is, don't ya? When they take that little—"

"Ah ah ah." I covered my ears with my hands. "I don't want to picture any part of that."

"I'm sorry, it just gets me all worked up is all." She patted her shirt, as if looking for something, then pulled out a thin silver stick. She stuck it in her mouth, a moment later exhaling a small cloud. "I just need to calm down."

I raised an eyebrow. "Is that...?"

"Legal from the state. For my anxiety. Helps me stay calm."

"That works?"

She grinned and slid the pen back in her pocket with a wink. "Like a charm."

"I only ever had it at parties in college. And I wasn't trying to stay calm then."

"Medical science is doing wonders." She closed her eyes and a slow smile formed. "What about this note, though? You calling the cops?"

I nodded. "I thought it could be important. And Nolan said I should. Then, I think we should try to talk to Marlene, Isaac, and Preston again."

"Good plan."

We walked to my office, and I sat to call the police. This time, I got Officer Longshore.

"Hello. Thea Pagoni again. I have something I think might be significant to the investigation."

He cleared his throat. "Uh, which investigation are you referring to?"

"The murder? At the campground?" Had he forgotten who I was?

"Oh, right. We're making good progress on that."

"Oh. You are? Do you have someone in custody?"

"Now, if you just called to get information out of me, I'll tell you right now, that's not going to happen. We already have enough going on with the press—"

"Officer Longshore, that's not why I'm calling."

"Okay then. What can I do for you?"

"Last night someone left a threatening note on my door, saying I could end up like Charlene."

There was a long pause and I heard papers rustling.

"Charlene, the murder victim?" I clarified.

"Yes, of course," he said. "And who gave you this note?"

"It was left on my cabin door."

"Uh huh. But you don't know by who?"

"How could I know that?" I breathed out slowly in exasperation. Hennie raised an eyebrow, probably confused by my end of the conversation.

"Well, I'll send someone to check it out and make a report, but there's no reason to think it's connected to the murder case."

"Except that the note mentioned the victim..." I pinched the bridge of my nose. With cops like Longshore and Randall, this thing would never get solved. "Is there still a detective working on the case? Maybe I should talk to him instead."

Longshore's tone grew sharp. "He's not taking calls at the moment. Busy solving the case, you see."

"Right. So, you'll send someone?"

"We'll get to it at some point today. We have a lot going on here, as you can imagine."

I could imagine nothing more than a large box of donuts and a bunch of small-town cops gossiping like ladies at the hair salon. This might be the first major crime most of them had encountered. Surely, the city detective would be more competent. I'd have to talk to Nolan later and see what he thought.

"Thank you for giving us a call," Longshore said. "Be sure to call back if anything else comes up."

"I will."

I set my phone down and shook my head at Hennie. "I hope nothing major ever happens to me in Outer Branson. I'd hate to rely on our PD for actual protection."

Hennie patted her side, where her holstered gun bulged. "That's why I don't."

I sighed. "Might need to get me one of those."

She grinned and let out a chuckle. "Who needs fire-power when you have a sexy man to do your protecting?"

I rolled my eyes but couldn't keep the smile from my face. "Nolan has other duties besides playing bodyguard."

"Is that what you were doing last night?" She moved her eyebrows up and down at me. "His 'other duties'"?

I looked down as my cheeks flushed. "We better check on that raccoon before we head out."

After feeding Ricky, we got into my car.

Nolan saw us and jogged over. "Where you heading?"

"Round two of interviews," I said.

He opened the back door and hopped in.

"Okay then." I drove off, pulling into Rollie's a few min-utes later.

I took a fresh notebook from the shelf while Hennie and Nolan chatted with Enid, catching her up. When I came to the register, Enid reached out and put her hand over mine.

"Now sweetie, I don't want you to get upset when I tell you this," she said.

I glanced sideways at Hennie and then Nolan.

"Some people are starting to... *talk*."

"About?" I asked.

"The campground. They don't think it's safe if a murder happened there."

I deflated with a sigh. "I know. We've had cancellations. And walk-in traffic is down. I don't know what to do."

"Solve this thing fast," Enid advised. "Faster it's over with, faster people will move on to the next big story."

"That's the truth," Hennie said. "They'll forget all about it by next month."

"I hope so." I paid and thanked Enid. "Oh, but I tried to make keftedakia last night and it didn't go well. It's just beef, onion, egg, and spices for the meatballs?"

"Well, the bread, of course. And the mint. Can't forget the mint. It's the most important ingredient besides the meat."

"Bread and mint," I mumbled to myself. She had left those out when she gave me the recipe. Hopefully nothing else was missing. "I'll give it another try." I jotted down a quick note for my next attempt. "Do you happen to know where Preston Bean lives?"

She nodded and excitement lit her eyes. "Are you going to bust him?"

I shook my head. "Nothing to bust yet. We're just going to ask more questions."

"Well, I think he's still in that old apartment building over on the north side of town."

"Thanks." I added the note to my page of information about Preston.

"Nice to see you again, Nolan," Enid said, waving her fingers at him.

He dipped his head to her. "And you."

"I am wondering, though..." Enid said to him. "When will you start using those connections of yours to solve this thing?"

"I don't have any connections."

"Lies." She waved him off. "We both know that's the furthest thing from the truth."

"Wait, a minute," I jumped in. "Do you have police connections?"

He held his hands up in protest. "I really don't, I just have some family members in the force, but I can't—"

"*Some* family members!" Enid exclaimed. "Only your own father and both brothers. And I know for a fact your dad would help because your aunt Rebecca asked me why you haven't called him yet. He's wondering himself."

"I can't do that," Nolan said.

"Why not!" I shrieked. "If it will help us solve this case and get the campground back on track, not to mention finding justice for a murder victim? Why won't you call him?"

He crossed his arms and gritted his teeth.

"I mean, it could be your job on the line," I said. "If this murder drags out long enough, we'll all be out of work."

"I know," he said.

"Surely, as a former cop, they'd give you the courtesy," Hennie added.

"I'm sure they would," he said.

"Then what's the problem?" I demanded.

He stared at me hard for a moment with a tight jaw, then swallowed and looked away. "They would use it against me," he admitted. "Say I made the wrong choice coming here. Try to bring me back. They're not exactly happy that I left the force or the city."

"Oh," I said. "I get that. I wouldn't want to be dragged into my past life, either."

He raised an eyebrow.

"My parents and sister cannot understand why I would leave corporate law to run a campground. I thought my parents, at least, would understand. But they always planned to sell the place off when Grandma and Grandad died."

"I'd say you made the right call," Nolan said.

"Maybe," I said. "If I don't end up shutting it down before the end of my first month."

"I think you'll figure it out," Nolan said.

"And you have me to help," Hennie added.

Enid nodded enthusiastically. "We have to find a way. For Bettie and Fish."

"For Grandma and Grandad," I agreed.

CHAPTER 10

We started with Marlene. This time when I knocked on the door, with two additional people at my side, she looked more shocked than annoyed. She wore too-tight workout pants and a top that looked painful in its constriction of her chest.

"You again?" She glared at me.

"I wondered if today might be a better time to sit and talk for a few minutes?" I asked.

"What would I want to do that for?" Marlene crossed her arms.

"I could sweeten the deal for you." Hennie reached into the small backpack that she carried in place of a purse and pulled out a tan cellophane-wrapped bar. "Hennie's Honey Facial Soap. I know you like that stuff."

Marlene narrowed her eyes, but snatched the bar from Hennie before stepping aside to let us in.

"Nice work," I whispered to Hennie as we entered the living room.

Clothing was scattered around the room, leaving no place to sit. A shirt and two dirty socks were on the coffee table beside many cups, plates, and bowls. The carpet might not have been vacuumed since it was installed. Clearly, Marlene was either depressed or just a terrible housekeeper.

I pushed aside a few articles of clothing to make a spot on the couch. Nolan stood near me, his arms crossed and his most serious face on. Hennie also opted to stand, but half leaned against the couch.

Marlene flopped into an armchair, not bothering to move the items out of the way first, and stared at us. "Let's get this over with."

"I was wondering about your alibi," I said. "You weren't at the campground that day?"

She crossed her arms. "What are you, the police now? Why should I tell you anything?"

"Because it was your sister? And because the faster this thing is solved, the sooner your name will be cleared as a suspect."

"I wasn't there," she snapped. "I was out shopping. I have the receipt and everything."

"Could we see it?" I asked.

"What'd ya buy?" Hennie added.

Marlene pushed herself up and stalked out of the room, then returned with a Victoria's Secret bag. I glanced at Nolan, whose cheeks had pinkened.

Marlene pulled out a receipt, then a thick, hooded sweatshirt.

I looked up at her. "You bought a hoodie at a lingerie store?"

"They sell plenty of stuff besides lingerie," Marlene said.

The receipt was dated for Monday, the day of the murder. Considering the purchase time and figuring in the distance the mall was from the campground, it seemed her alibi held up.

"What do you know about the note I received last night?" I asked.

"Note? I don't know nothing about any note."

"It warned that I would be killed if I kept asking questions," I said.

"Well, I ain't in no condition to harm anyone. I wouldn't risk my baby like that." She dropped her hand to her stomach.

"Baby?" I exchanged shocked glances with Hennie and Nolan. "Who are you having a baby with?"

"His name is Sam, not that it's any of your business." She turned her nose up and added, "He loves me and we're going to be married."

"Well, that's... Congratulations." Maybe my jealousy theory didn't hold up after all.

I thought of my next question as my gaze traveled around the room. Before I could say more, I caught a glimpse of something that made my heart skip.

I recognized the colors first. I'd stared at the larger version of the Cedar Fish Campground map for all of my life with its mint green background. Some writing was visible, but the map was tucked under a stack of magazines and mail.

I made myself cough several times while choking out, "Could I have some water?"

Marlene rolled her eyes but got up and trudged into the kitchen. When she was out of sight, I stopped coughing and slid the map out of the pile. I tucked it into my purse but didn't have time to address Hennie's and Nolan's questioning stares before Marlene returned.

"Thanks." I sipped the water but didn't drink much. Who knew how dirty the glass was. "You said before that Isaac was stalking Charlene. Do you have any evidence of that?"

"Nope. I'm sure there's messages on her phone, but the cops have that."

"What about Preston?" Nolan asked. "Do you think he could be involved in any way? Had they been arguing or having trouble in their relationship?"

"No," Marlene said with a pout. "He loved Charlene and only Charlene."

Maybe Marlene had hooked up with Sam to make Preston jealous. Or maybe Sam was her consolation prize for failing to win Preston over. Good stuff for a soap opera, but it didn't help me figure out who killed Charlene.

"Do you still think Isaac killed her?" I asked.

She blew out a huffy breath. "Don't know who else it could be. He's crazy, and he's been coming around a lot lately, which I don't like. I'm not going to be his Charlene replacement, if that's what he's thinking. Never could compare to her anyhow."

I pondered her resentment. I wasn't a twin, and my sister and I had both been successful in our own separate endeavors. I never felt jealous of her, but I could guess that living with the feeling that your identical twin somehow outdid you, couldn't be easy. With pregnancy hormones on the rampage, Marlene might've had a bad night and decided to end their sisterly competition by being the last one standing, literally.

"Thank you, Marlene." I stood, and Hennie and Nolan followed me to the door. "I wish you the best with Sam and the baby."

We piled into the car, and once we had driven out of sight, I pulled out the map and thrust it at Hennie, who sat in the passenger seat. "What's written on it?"

"Just a circle around where it points to the overlook."

I gaped at her for a moment before returning my eyes to the road. "Nolan?"

"I see it." He had leaned over the backseat to look at the map.

"Well?" I demanded.

"It's interesting," he said. "Doesn't make her look more innocent, that's for sure."

"And you never did see two sisters hate each other more," Hennie said. "Everyone knew it."

"Her jealousy and coldness..." I glanced at them. "I'm thinking that Isaac was either in the wrong place at the wrong time and got framed, or he and Marlene were in on this together. Oh!" In my excitement, I reached over and grabbed Hennie's arm. "What if the couple people saw was actually Marlene and Isaac instead of Charlene and Isaac?"

"Hard to tell the difference if they're twins," Nolan said.

"And today Marlene was wearing athletic pants like Charlene did. They might have had the same color leggings."

"Twins do like to dress alike," Hennie said.

I nodded. "Maybe Preston will give us more."

We found his building easily, since it was the only apartment building on that end of town. Next to the front door, Preston's name was listed beside 2C for the buzzer system. I pressed the button, but nothing happened. Nolan pulled on the door and found it unlocked. We walked up to the second floor and knocked on 2C.

Preston opened the door a crack, saw me, and glared. "Yeah?"

"I was hoping we could talk for a minute?"

"I'm busy and I have nothing to say."

I glanced over at Hennie and Nolan. Hennie shrugged. Nolan straightened up and moved closer to me. I guess it would be too easy if Hennie had a magical soap bar that could persuade all of our interviewees to talk.

"Did you love Charlene?" I shouted as he closed the door.

The door opened, this time, revealing Preston's full head. "Yes, of course. And you don't need to be out here yelling about it."

"We did ask to come in," I pointed out.

I looked behind him into the small piece of the living room that was visible. I didn't see much besides the end of a couch and a light from a TV. On the wall, a purse, two jackets, and a sweatshirt hung on hooks. A jolt of excitement leapt through me. The blue hoodie had a brown-orange smudge on the sleeve that had to be from cheese curls. Though, the more I looked at it, I realized it was too brown to be cheese. Probably just dirt.

The only other thing of interest I noted was that the two jackets seemed to belong to women: one featured pink buttons and the other, a floral lining. Could they both be Charlene's? Could one be Charlene's and the other Marlene's? What did it mean that a purse was hanging there, as well?

"Well, you ain't coming in," Preston said.

I went for the bold option. "If you loved her, why did you kill her?"

"I didn't! I told you, I was working all day, and my uncle can back that up. I planned to propose to Charlene. Opposite of killing her, you see? I wanted to spend my life with her." His words had a sharp, angry edge.

A woman's voice called out from the part of the couch not visible to me. "Don't get yourself all worked up, baby."

Preston looked over at her and back to me with a smug expression.

"I see that you're really mourning the loss of your almost fiancée," I said. That explained the purse and at least one of the jackets.

"We all grieve in different ways." Preston shut the door and the chain rattled.

I turned to Nolan and Hennie. "That was interesting."

"I'll say." Hennie rocked back on her heels. "Now what?"

I looked to Nolan, who glared at the door.

"What do you think?" I asked him.

"Let's go." He kept one eye on the door as we walked away.

Back in the car, I relayed what I'd seen and my thoughts.

"He's a prime suspect," Nolan said. "Something about his demeanor."

"Gives me the willies," Hennie added.

"Being creepy doesn't make someone a murderer," I said. "People always say it's the ones you don't expect. I still think Isaac is squirrelly enough to have done it, and Marlene is certainly cold enough. Maybe they all worked together."

"Unlikely," Nolan said.

"But wouldn't that be the way to trick the police?" I said. "Do something unlikely to throw them off?"

"I guess it would be pretty genius," Nolan agreed.

"Ain't none of them smart enough for something like that," Hennie said.

I had no further conclusions by the time I pulled back into Cedar Fish. I drove slowly down the main loop to Isaac's campsite. We got out and looked around, but the site was clear of any personal belongings. In fact, it was clear of most natural debris as well. Even the fire ring looked like it had been washed.

"I thought he was on the books for one more night." I took out my phone and dialed the main office.

After eight rings, Curtis finally answered with a slow, "Cedar Fish Campground. How can I help you today?"

"It's Thea. Did Isaac Lang check out?"

"I'll check." I heard a page turn. Then another. Then another.

"He was here yesterday," I added, "so it would have been this morning, maybe?"

"Oh. Young man?"

"Yes. Brown, kinda wild hair?"

"Said he was leaving early."

"So, he did check out," I clarified.

"Yes, ma'am."

"Did you forget that I asked you to tell me immediately when Isaac checked out?"

There was a long pause, and then, "Yes, ma'am."

I sighed. "Thanks, Curtis."

I ended the call and threw my hands up in exasperation. "Isaac checked out and Curtis forgot to tell me."

"Hey, come here and have a look-see." Hennie poked a stick into nearby brush.

A scrap of paper was caught in the twigs, just far enough into the bush that Isaac must've missed it when he was cleaning up.

I looked to Nolan. "Okay to touch it?"

"This isn't a crime scene," he said.

Hennie added, "Yet."

I bent down and pulled the paper free, then stood to read it. "Even if you don't feel the same, I want you to know how much I love—" I handed the note to Nolan. "Unless they were having an intense discussion over favorite pizza toppings, I'd say this comes off a bit stalkery, don't you think?"

Hennie nodded.

"We don't know who wrote it," Nolan said. "It could have been here before Isaac."

"Good point. I do have Isaac's handwriting on the check-in form."

"Lookey here." Hennie pointed to a tree.

Initials were carved into the bark in sharp, jagged letters: "IL + CK 4E."

"Why would he carve that if she's dead?" Hennie asked.

"Or if she was with someone else?" Nolan asked.

"I think he was in denial about Charlene and Preston," I said. "Maybe he did it before she died. Or maybe he likes to deface campground property."

Nolan gestured to the spotless site. "Not likely."

"Well, it was definitely him," I said. "He just left, and who else would have the initials IL and CK except Isaac Lang and Charlene Kirby?"

"He did say he tries to be romantic," Hennie added.

"This is more creepy than romantic," I said. "Let's get out of here."

We rode back to the office, and I dug through the file cabinet to find the form.

I laid the form and the note on the counter side-by-side.

I squinted at the Os and then the Is. "Looks like a match to me."

"Definitely," Hennie said.

"Where's the note that was taped to your door?" Nolan asked.

"Oh! Good idea!" I'd been so freaked out when the note showed up that I hadn't thought about having Isaac's handwriting nearby.

I hurried out of the office, dashed to my cabin, fed Ricky as quickly as possible, and jogged back to the office, note in hand. Breathing hard, I spread the note out beside the other papers. Immediately, it was clear the handwriting did not match. The threatening note was written with sharper letters, the Os looking more like ovals than circles, and all with a slight slant.

Hennie had taken off in my absence, so I turned to Nolan.

"Isaac definitely didn't write the note. Do we call the cops and tell them what we found at Isaac's site?" I asked.

"Wouldn't hurt," Nolan said. "If he's still a suspect, they should at least come out and look at it."

I entered my office to call the police, but as I reached for the phone, I noticed that Curtis had set today's *Outer Branson Daily News* on my desk. The front headline, loud and huge over a photo featuring the Cedar Fish Campground sign, read, "Most Dangerous Campground in the Country."

I quickly skimmed through the article, my heart pounding faster with each paragraph. The whole story explained how my campground had a history of violence, which was really a list of the few accidents that had happened over the last fifty years. It said there was no security—also untrue—and that having a murder on its grounds made it the most dangerous campground in the country. That couldn't be true, either.

I turned on my laptop, went to Google, and frantically typed. Several articles came up under "dangerous campgrounds." The campground with the most deaths was said to have multiple deaths per year. Far more than Cedar Fish. Even when I searched "campground murders," I found—to my horror—that campground murders were not at all unique, and there had even been a serial killer who'd murdered ten people in a two-year span.

I snatched my phone up, but instead of dialing the police, I called the newspaper.

I was still on hold when Curtis yelled my name. I couldn't hang up after holding for so long. "Yes?" I called back.

"Police are here to see you," he said.

Nice timing. I growled as I hung up and walked out front to greet Officer Randall.

He pulled up his belt as he nodded. "I'm here to take your report."

Good thing I hadn't been in any real danger, since it took him most of the day to get there. "Right. I'll get the note." I retrieved it from my desk and handed it over. "It was taped to my cabin door."

"And you touched it," Randall said. "Probably ruined any fingerprints we might've gotten from it." He gave me a displeased look.

"I didn't think you'd do that."

"I guess that's why you're not an officer and I am."

I gritted my teeth and forced a slow breath out through my nose. "How is the murder investigation going? Made any arrests yet?"

He glanced at me, then back at the note. "Not yet, but we're getting closer."

"Really? Who's your prime suspect?"

He handed me a clipboard. "You'll need to fill this out with as much detail as possible."

"We also found this note at Isaac's campsite after he checked out. It matches Isaac's handwriting, and I think it shows proof he was stalking Charlene." I slid the second note and Isaac's check-in form toward him before walking away.

I sat in my office and hurriedly scribbled down the details of what had happened the night before.

"You'll look into this?" I handed the clipboard back. "I think it might've been Preston or Marlene since the handwriting doesn't match Isaac's."

"Now look, Miss Pagoni, you've been warned about getting involved in this case. Let the police do their job, and stay out of the way."

I crossed my arms. "It'd be much easier to do that if I felt like you were actually making progress. But I seem to be finding out more than you."

His face fell into a stiff, unamused expression. "I don't tell you how to run your campground—though it doesn't look like you're doing too hot of a job, if you've seen the papers. Don't tell us how to do our jobs."

But you're not doing it at all! I forced a smile and said, "Thanks for taking my statement. I'm sure you'll do all you can to find out who wrote it and threatened to kill me."

"Let's just hope they don't come back and finish the job."

I swallowed hard and my hands tightened into fists. I'd never dealt with such an incompetent jerk in all my life.

Several possible comebacks ran through my mind, but all of them would be too antagonistic.

"Luckily, we do have a security guard on the premises. Thank you for your concern," I added sarcastically.

He took the clipboard but left the notes. Maybe he'd taken photos when I was filling out my statement, but I doubted it. It was like they didn't even care about the evidence.

After Randall walked out, I slammed my office door shut and picked up my phone again, listening to the now-familiar hold message of the *Outer Branson Daily News*.

Chapter 11

"Fine, I'll wait again." I tapped my foot and crunched a piece of ice. Ricky looked up at me from his cage on my office floor.

When the woman at the police station came back on the line, she asked, "Who were you holding for?"

"I need to talk to someone about pressing charges against a newspaper for printing false information and refusing to correct it."

"Oh, right. Hold please."

I growled at the syrupy hold music. My weekend hadn't been the best, and now that it was Monday morning again, it was time to get things done. The paper couldn't get away with printing information that was flat-out wrong and would damage my business. I had even stooped to writing a letter—on letterhead I'd just created—from the "law offices" of Thea Pagoni, threatening a lawsuit for libel.

The line clicked and the hold music stopped. "Ma'am? We can have you file a report, and it'll be processed in our main office," the woman said.

"Fine. I just need a case number for my paperwork."

I took the information and planned to stop by the police station on my trip into town for supplies.

Before I headed out, I checked my email one last time and narrowed my eyes at a message from the *Outer Branson Daily News*. I opened it and almost choked on the flowery sentiment.

"Miss Pagoni, please accept our most humble of apologies. Our business is to tell the truth and only the truth, and we never aim to harm businesses. We sincerely regret that we have caused you distress. We have printed a retraction in today's paper, in accordance with the letter we received. We expect this retraction and apology will satisfy your demands."

I huffed. They made it sound like I'd sent them a ransom note. I stood and leaned into the main office. "Curtis? Have the papers come yet?"

He swept his head in a slow circle until he could see the front door. "Yep."

I slid the top paper from the bundle and took it to my office. Nothing on the front page. I spread it open on the desk and scanned article after article. Finally, way in the back, all the way at the bottom, there was a section titled, "Retractions."

A few items were listed. One name had been misspelled in an obituary. A wedding announcement listed the incorrect date. And last on the list, "A misprint in Friday's paper claimed Cedar Fish Campground as the most dangerous in the country. We have since found new information proving this to be false."

I shut the paper with a *thwack* and stuffed it into the trashcan, growling as I punched it farther in and kept punching.

Ricky chattered beside me, banging on his bars with his water dish and yanking on the door.

"I understand the need to get out your anger," Nolan said, suddenly appearing in my office doorway, "but you're going to hurt your hand doing it like that."

I squealed in surprise and jumped, smoothing my hair down and trying to slow my breath. "They printed the retraction."

He nodded knowingly. "Never quite undoes the damage, does it?"

"Not when they print the false information on the front page, above the fold, and the retraction is on one of the last pages in a tiny box. I could make an argument in court that it was not an equal comparison to the original misprint and therefore, doesn't count."

Nolan bravely pulled the paper from the can and looked where I pointed. "That's ludicrous," he agreed.

"It's going to destroy us. I don't know what to do. Even suing the paper won't fix the bad press we've already gotten."

"Maybe some... better SEO?" He shrugged.

"I don't think that will help much."

"I don't know. I always hear people saying they need to have better SEO to get more business, but I have no idea what that means."

I chuckled and it broke the angry tension. "Search Engine Optimization. It's what makes a website pop up higher on the list in search results."

"Oh. No, I guess that wouldn't help us much."

"Well, maybe. We could draw in a younger crowd if we hit them where they are—online. It's not a bad idea."

"I came to show you this." He handed me a stack of square photos, some crinkled and half burned. "These were left behind in the young adults' campsite."

I recognized them as similar to the photo we'd found at the crime scene. In these shots, a slightly blurred young man in a red jacket stood as the focal point.

"Guess that explains the red streak in the photo we found." I sighed and plopped down in my chair. "So that clue means nothing. It wasn't the killer."

"Doesn't look like it."

"Unless the killer was one of the young adults?" I sat up and raised my eyebrows at him.

Nolan shook his head.

I sighed. "This is hopeless. This murder is never going to get solved. I gave up my whole life to come here, to start over, and now it's all falling apart." My heart sped and my chest tightened. The room started to waiver at the edges. "Where's my ice!" I snatched the mug from my desk and chomped hard on a big cube. It cracked into pieces, and the cold seeped into my teeth. I focused on the sensation.

"I'm sorry. I don't know what to say." Nolan leaned on the doorframe, a defeated look on his face. "I'd love to tell you it'll be solved soon, and that business will pick up, and it'll all be alright. But I'm not the sort to sugarcoat. It looks bad, Thea. And I don't know how to help you fix it."

I rubbed my forehead and chomped the rest of the ice cube. "I don't expect you to. But thank you for wanting to."

"Purely for selfish reasons." He hesitated, then added, "There is one thing I could do..."

"What's that?"

"I don't have a computer, though. Decided to get away from that world, so I'd have to use yours, if that's okay."

I stood up and gestured to the chair in front of my laptop. "By all means."

I watched over his shoulder as he typed in a web address and logged in.

"What!" I smacked his shoulder. "You've had access to the police database this whole time and you're just now telling me?!"

He gave a half smile and kept typing. "I don't have access, but my dad and brothers do. And I remembered that

I had one of their logins. But, understand, the information is going to be limited, and this isn't technically legal. This is the global database, so it won't have the most up-to-date information from the local police databases."

We watched the page load, lines of text and photos being revealed inch by inch.

Nolan sighed. "Of course, at this rate, the database might be updated before I can even get to it."

"Yeah, our internet isn't exactly the fastest," I said. "But hey, we offer free Wi-Fi, and that's the most important part."

Nolan looked at the half-loaded page and then back to me. "Uh huh." He nodded toward Ricky and asked, "What's going on with the little bandit?"

"He was getting too agitated being alone in my cabin all day."

Nolan raised an eyebrow and turned back to the computer screen.

When the page finished loading, we clicked and scrolled through the case file. The information on the suspects and persons of interest was the most informative.

"So, Preston's uncle lied?" I gaped at the note on the screen.

Nolan whistled. "Man, that's huge."

"Is it?"

"Lying about an alibi?" He shot a look over his shoulder. "Yeah. It's a big deal."

"Oh, but look." I pointed to Marlene's name. "Marlene's alibi checked out." A still of Marlene from a store video camera was attached that showed the time and day of when the murder was suspected to have taken place.

"I don't know what to think now," I admitted. "Isaac still seems guilty to me, but I was sure Marlene did it after we talked to her, and Preston seemed to have an alibi, but now..."

Nolan logged out and turned to face me, stroking his beard with one hand. "I'm thinking that if he lied about his alibi, it's got to be Preston."

"It's looking more like it every day."

The phone rang. I looked to see if Curtis was going to answer. He moved so slowly toward the phone that I grew impatient and snatched the receiver to my ear.

"Cedar Fish Campground, how can I help you?"

"Help!" a woman shrieked, then whispered, "There's a baby bear!"

My eyes widened and I put the call on speakerphone. "Can you tell us where you saw the bear?"

Nolan listened in beside me. The woman described a picnic area near the river.

As soon as she hung up, Nolan said, "I'm on it."

"Be careful!"

I paced my office floor, wanting to follow him to help, but wanting more to avoid the bear, even if it was only a cub. "We should have pepper spray," I muttered to myself.

"Where is Hennie and her shotgun when I need her?" I had gotten used to her hanging around most days.

My phone rang with Nolan's number. I answered, "Are you okay?"

On the other end, he laughed. "You have got to come see this."

"Did you find the bear?"

"Yup. Hurry and get over here."

"I don't want to come if there's a bear!"

Nolan sighed. "Can you trust me?"

"Fine." I hung up and grabbed my keys, driving along the main road to the larger loop, where the picnic area was.

I got out and saw Nolan standing near a family of five. All of them watched the water, where a black, hairy creature splashed on the rocks.

Nolan turned and waved me over, then pointed to the "bear."

He did look very much like a tiny bear. Had I stumbled upon him unexpectedly, I would have drawn the same conclusion. As we watched, the black Newfoundland puppy stood up with a gar flopping in his mouth.

The kids shrieked in joy and the dad recorded video. Then, a chorus of, "Can we keep him?" rang out in whiny cries.

The parents, adamant in their refusal, eventually turned to me for help.

"I'm sure he belongs to someone," I said. "That's an expensive breed."

"See kids," the mom said gratefully, "he has a home already, and he's lost. They're going to help find his family." She smiled at me.

"Right. I'll put up flyers," I said.

The family left and I looked to Nolan. "Now what?"

Nolan inched closer and knelt down, then called to the dog. The gar flopped out of the puppy's mouth. He batted the water, but when the fish was out of reach, he turned his attention to Nolan. After staring at him for several moments, the dog sat down in the water.

I whistled and tapped my thigh twice. The puppy perked his ears, then bounded over to me, tongue lolling happily out of his mouth. He licked my arm and panted at me.

"Nicely done," Nolan said. "No collar."

"Hmm." I looked over the dog's matted hair. Pieces of leaves and twigs were stuck in clumps with mud. A small patch of missing hair on his back revealed raw, red skin underneath. "He's been out here a while."

"He seems trained," Nolan pointed out. "Must've gotten lost somewhere far away."

I petted the puppy's head. "I guess you're hanging out with me until we find your owner." He barked once in agreement.

When I opened my back car door and called, "Come on," the dog promptly hopped into the backseat. His wet, dirty hair made spots all over the upholstery. Irritation ran through my veins, but there was little I could do. I should have known that bringing a Lexus to a campground would be a bad idea. The paints had gotten scratched when I tried to drive down an overgrown road, and inside and out held a constant layer of dirt.

The puppy stretched out, taking up the entire backseat, and looked at me. His cheerfulness faded my annoyance. When we got back to the office, the puppy followed us out of the car. I opened the office door and saw chaos.

Curtis's stool lay on its side. Several items had fallen from the shelves. Papers were scattered, and I heard scampering somewhere I couldn't identify.

Nolan stiffened at my side. "Stay here."

He crept along an aisle. The scampering grew louder and then Ricky dashed in front of Nolan, coming straight at me. The raccoon saw the dog and halted, chattering his complaint over my new friend.

Curtis rounded the corner, moving faster than I'd ever seen, at a crawling pace. "I tried to catch him."

"I'll get the cage," Nolan said.

I snatched Ricky up and cradled him like a baby.

"Slight problem." Nolan held up the cage, the door hanging loose from one hinge.

"He busted out," Curtis explained.

"You little rascal," I scolded him.

"Wild animals need to be outdoors," Curtis hollered.

"I know," I said. "But he's still too little."

Ricky pushed out of my arms and dashed away.

"Ricky!" I called.

Curtis opened the front and held it.

"What are you doing?" I asked.

He pointed accusingly at me.

"Close the door!"

Ricky rushed around the corner and made for his freedom. Dill bolted from the shadows and chased after him. For an instant, I was distracted in wondering where it was Dill hung out all day and how she managed to run so fast being such an old cat. When Ricky sprinted past me, out the door, I ran after him, calling his name. Dill dashed outside, too, and disappeared into a bush.

I charged around, trying to see movement. Ricky was little, but not tiny. I frantically searched, to no avail. When I gave up, after several minutes without a hint of his whereabouts, I turned to find Nolan, Curtis, and the puppy sitting in front of the building, watching me.

"Help," I pleaded.

Nolan shook his head. Curtis waved me off and made his way back inside.

"He's too little! He'll die!"

"I think he'll be fine," Nolan said.

"How can you say that! He's been drinking from the bottle every few hours."

Nolan held back a laugh. "I don't think that was because he needed to be bottle fed."

"What are you saying?" I put my hands on my hips.

"That he's maybe been milking it a bit."

I looked behind me one last time. "I'm worried about him."

"He is a wild animal."

"Everyone keeps saying that."

CHAPTER 12

I hadn't been sleeping well, so when I woke early on Tuesday morning, I decided to get a jump on the day rather than toss and turn in bed. I sat on my porch, notebook in hand, reviewing all the clues and facts. The puppy, who'd I started calling Gar, lay at my feet, tied to a make-shift collar and leash. I'd spent hours last night washing him, removing the debris from his hair, and combing out knots. He looked like a new dog today.

I looked over what I'd written since my investigation started. From the beginning, Isaac had looked guilty. The way he came running out of the trail, the fact that he was the one seen there that day, and the note we'd found in his campsite all pointed to him being the killer. The note threatening me hadn't matched Isaac's handwriting, though. Also, the only person claiming to see Preston that day was Isaac. Marlene's jealousy and coldness were a factor. Her alibi might have held up, but that didn't mean she wasn't in on it somehow. Her marking the overlook on the map and calling about the trail made her highly suspicious. And Preston. If he was innocent, why lie about his alibi? Something wasn't right about him. As far as I could see, all three of them looked equally guilty and innocent.

I thought Gar and I could both use a walk, so, in the still-sleeping campground, in the grey of the morning, we made our way down the path. Fog filled low areas and insects sang along with the birds. I found it to be the most peaceful time of the day—before the world woke up and disturbed the precious morning's pearl. Pink sunrise streaks peeked through the trees.

I picked out specific sounds: the light crunch of my sneakers and Gar's paws on the dirt road, crickets congregating at the pond and lake, and the warbling song of a whip-or-will. I looked up and found a bird's nest with a security camera pointed at it. Our one working camera.

I huffed in frustration but realized something. The camera, though aimed at the nest, was still pointed in the direction of the north hiking trail's entrance. There might be a chance the trail was visible in the background of the shot.

Gar followed me back to the office, chasing a bunny along the way, and I pulled out the videotape from the day of the murder. Now I felt grateful for the instinct I had felt to keep it. I popped the tape in and leaned close to the screen.

A sliver of the trail's entrance could be seen through the leaves of the tree. I zoomed ahead on the tape and gasped when I saw Charlene. Her bright purple pants streaked past the camera just long enough for me to make out her face. I rewound and watched a few more times. She was alone, but it was only seconds later that Isaac followed her.

I thought back to the camper who'd told me she'd seen a couple. Could she have meant Isaac and Charlene if they hadn't entered the trail at the same time? A short while later, the group of young adults appeared. I made myself watch to the point where Hennie and I entered the trail with the police. No one unexpected showed up.

If I'd been thinking that Preston or Marlene had some-how snuck in and followed Charlene on the trail, this proved that neither of them had been there. The police had done a thorough check of the grounds and said they found no evidence of a disturbance that might indicate someone had made their own way to the trail.

I returned to my original conclusion. I should have trusted my gut from the start. Isaac was the most logical, reasonable, obvious answer. It had to be him.

I wandered out to get the paper. The front headline read, "No Justice at Murder Fish Campground." It wasn't a story about the campground, so much as the police's inability to make real progress on the case. But it didn't make the campground look very good, either.

I paged through our reservation book. Many names had been crossed out. Few remained. Even if I knew Isaac had done it, it didn't matter. The video didn't show much we hadn't already known, though the police might still want to see it. From what the article in the paper said, the police hadn't found enough evidence to arrest anyone, nor did they have a solid lead.

I clicked back in my history to the police database site. I'd hoped that Nolan's login would still be active, but, of course, he'd been timed out. I clicked over to my inbox, and my stomach tightened when I saw the email from the lawyer.

I'd been waiting to hear from him about the estate settlement for so long that I'd almost forgotten. But this would tell me how much money I had to put into the campground. Nolan and I had calculated something around $20,000 for all the repairs. It would take at least a few thousand in advertising to bring in enough business to keep going. Anything left would go toward making needed improvements.

I held my breath and opened the email. I scanned quickly through his small talk and found the number. I'd hoped for something like $50,000 at least. That would make this new life of mine work. The number the lawyer had listed, which he promised would be wired to the business account within days, was only $16,842.

I blinked at the number and reread the sentence three times. Not even enough for the necessary things. I swallowed hard and opened my bank account website. In my personal savings, I had a few thousand, but not enough for me to start taking anything from it. If things went under,

I'd need that little cushion to fall back on until I could figure out my next step. My only other asset was my car. I'd
already been thinking of selling it before it got anymore
beat up. I could buy a cheap truck—something better suit-
ed for a campground than a shiny Lexus. That would bring
in a few thousand, but hardly anything substantial.

The tears burned my throat and I closed my eyes a moment to breathe. Somehow, I would make it work. Maybe
not all repairs needed to be done right away. Maybe only a
few hundred in advertising could get reservations coming
in.

The list of repairs sat on my desk, and I reviewed it
again. The pool would still have to be drained, cleaned,
and repainted. No way around that—it was too critical of
an amenity. But the paint peeling from the siding of the
office and rec hall might have to wait, and if the roofs
couldn't last one more season before being patched, then
the playground would have to remain swingless and a few
toilets would have to remain cracked. With so little money
coming in, I'd also have to supplement my employees' payroll with the estate's settlement. We needed a pool maintenance person, and it was starting to look like that might
be me.

My workday droned on, mostly consisting of paperwork
for the lawyer and other things that kept being pushed
aside to solve the murder. Every time I sighed or growled
under my breath in frustration, Gar would wake from his
nap long enough to roll over and press his back against

me or nudge me with his wet nose. His presence felt nice, though the dread at knowing I had to find his owners ate at me.

I needed a break so badly that I texted Hennie, "What are you up to today?"

Instead of texting back, she called me. When I answered, I heard the noise of a crowd in the background.

"I'm at a honey convention in the big city," Hennie explained.

"St. Louis?"

"No, Branson."

I held back my laughter. Outer Branson was small in population, and Branson wasn't much bigger. Neither were anything close to a "big city" by my definition. "Sounds busy."

"People love their honey. I'm making a killing!"

"Good."

"How's our investigation?" she asked.

"Meh." I shrugged even though she couldn't see it. "A few things have happened."

I explained about the newspaper fiasco, my frustration with the police, Preston lying about his alibi, finding Gar, and the video camera footage. I left out the part about Ricky breaking free—I still hadn't found him, and I didn't want her to worry.

"I missed a lot in a few days," she said.

"How long is this convention?"

"I'll be back tomorrow, don't you worry. We'll get this thing solved."

"I hope so."

After we hung up, I took Gar outside to go to the bathroom. He'd been cooped up far too long and bolted around the building at full speed several times, pausing each time he reached me to yip and loll his tongue and spin around before charging off again. When he'd burned off some energy, I was able to take his photo.

After dragging Gar back inside, I made a simple poster with his photo and a number to call. I opened the Print screen and stared at the quantity box. He didn't have a collar. No one had called or come looking for him. It'd taken me hours to comb the mats out of his fur and get him cleaned up. Gar didn't seem sad or lonely, like he was missing his family. He seemed happy to be with me, like he'd been found. Or maybe I'd imagined it because it felt so good that he'd found me.

I selfishly typed in 2 and clicked Print. I hung the posters—one in the office, and one in the rec hall.

When Nolan saw the poster behind the front counter, he held back a laugh. "Effective."

"What?" I snapped. I looked again at my poster. So what if it wasn't the most visible? "People can see it."

He patted Gar and smiled. "I'm calling it a day. I think I found a solution for the pool. Just have to get the pump I found running again. I think I can get it drained tomorrow."

"Perfect. Thank you."

I headed home that evening with Gar at my side. It felt so natural and so normal and so *right* that I decided if Gar's family did turn up and he left, I would get myself a dog. And if his family didn't turn up, then I already had one.

Gar stopped suddenly in front of me and growled at the cabin. We were still behind it, coming up the back path from the pool area.

"What is it?" I asked Gar.

I inched slowly around the corner and saw the screen door torn to shreds. I sucked in a breath and took several huge steps back. Gar pressed himself against my side as I called Nolan.

He arrived quickly and pulled out his gun to sweep the front door. The door was still locked. He went around to the back door and found it still locked, too. I noticed the window in the living room was open. I hadn't shut it before I went to bed last night.

"The window." I pointed.

Nolan peeked in and watched a moment. Then, he tucked his gun back in his belt holster and crossed his arms as he faced me. "I see who's in there."

"Who? And why aren't you—?" Then I had a thought. "Uh oh."

"Come see."

I stood beside him at the window and surveyed the damage to my living room. It looked like it had been tossed by a burglar. Broken candle and books on the floor, lamp smashed, couch cushion torn, food scattered over the floor. And, sitting in the middle of the kitchen, surrounded by torn boxes and bags, Ricky stuffed his tiny mouth with potato chips and mini Reese's peanut butter cups.

"Ricky! What have you done?"

He snapped his head in my direction and squawked before throwing an apple core.

I turned to Nolan with a sheepish smile. "At least it wasn't a murderer who came to try to kill me, right?"

He laughed. "I don't know. That raccoon could suffocate you in your sleep. And rabies is rather fatal."

"Ricky would never do that, and he doesn't have rabies!" I glanced back inside the house where Ricky had climbed onto the kitchen counter. He found a package of jerky and ripped it open, then stuffed chunks of dried meat into his mouth. "That was my favorite jerky."

Nolan raised an eyebrow. "Store-bought stuff?"

"What other option is there?"

"City girl," he muttered.

I smacked his arm playfully. "You're one to talk! You used to live ten minutes from my duplex."

"Really?"

I nodded. "You listed your previous address on your application, and I recognized it. I lived by the Spring Street Park."

"That is close. Yet we had to come all the way out here to meet."

I thought of the one occasion I'd called the police from that house. Had it been a different day, maybe Nolan would have shown up and taken my statement. An icy rush slid through my veins and I shivered.

"Guess we better get him out of there," Nolan said.

I handed him my keys. "Good luck!"

Nolan left the door open, and a few minutes later, Ricky scampered out. I held Gar's rope leash tight as he growled and barked at Ricky.

We walked in to survey the damage.

"This is the perfect end to a horrible day." My throat burned and I closed my eyes to breathe.

"Something happen?"

"No, and that's the problem. This murder case doesn't seem to be moving along, and the cancellations are building up. I've been counting on the settlement from the estate to cover revamping the place, but I found out today that it's nowhere near enough."

"I'd hate to see this place close, for your sake and for mine. I like it here. A lot."

"Me too." I blinked and a tear rolled down my cheek. I swiped it away.

"I wish I could do something to help you," he said. "If you need to skip a few paychecks, I understand. If there's anything else I can do..."

"I can't have you do that. You're already getting paid next to nothing."

"I don't have many expenses, and I have some money saved up."

I sunk into the armchair, rubbed my forehead, and groaned, "I need ice."

Before I could stand up to get it, Nolan had pulled the ice cube tray from the freezer, popped a few cubes into a mug and refilled the now-empty spots. He held the mug out to me, and I took it with wide eyes.

"What was that?" I asked.

"What do you mean?"

"You got me ice and refilled the ice cube tray."

"Should I not have...?"

"But I didn't even ask you to," I pointed out.

He quirked an eyebrow at me. "You said you wanted ice. And refilling the tray is what you do when you take the frozen cubes out."

"It is." I smiled despite myself. "And you'd think it would be that obvious to anyone, right?"

He nodded slowly. "Ahh. Your ex?"

"Refused to refill it. Got so mad one night at my nagging over it—" I caught myself before I said too much. But Nolan hadn't missed it.

"You fought over the ice cube tray?" he asked.

"We more than fought over it."

The memory flashed in my mind: me snapping at Russell, him throwing the ice cube tray at my head, me laughing—until he slapped me. I shook the image away before the memory went any further.

Nolan studied my expression and seemed to make a decision. "I figured out a long time ago that if I didn't want to be nagged, I needed to do my part without being asked. I'm not a child. I should be able to keep up with a house like an adult."

"Easier said than done some days."

"Easier these days."

I nodded. "It's simpler here. But life is still complicated and messy." I nudged a leaking box of Cornflakes with my toe and picked up my grandma's crystal vase. "At least this didn't get broken."

"I may not be able to help with the mess of life, but I can help you clean this up." Nolan stooped to pick up the empty bag of Ruffles.

I waved it off. "Just leave it. I don't even care anymore."

"Not true." He swept bits of a shattered mug from the counter into his hand and dumped them into the trash. "Point me to a broom."

I pointed and got to work myself. With two of us tackling the anarchy together, the place cleaned up fast. When things were mostly back in order, I addressed the torn couch. "Guess I needed to replace this old thing anyhow." I rubbed my finger over the little cream bumps in the fabric.

"Maybe it can be sewn," Nolan said.

"Maybe, but I doubt it's worth it. I hate to get rid of anything that was Grandad and Grandma's, but I guess keeping a torn-up couch won't bring them back."

He looked up at me with a sad smile. "Nothing ever does."

"Thanks for your help." I felt nervous suddenly, talking to him.

"Glad to be able to do something."

"You've done a lot. I'm so grateful that you answered that ad. I wouldn't feel safe at all if I didn't know you were so close."

He gave a long, slow smile and dipped his head at me. "Glad to be of service, ma'am."

CHAPTER 13

In the morning, I double checked all of the windows before leaving the house. As much as I wanted to provide a safe place for Ricky, I didn't want him tearing my cabin up again. I let Gar out and locked up, but when I turned back around, I saw only his tail as Gar took off.

I chased after him until I lost my breath and panted as I continued to walk, calling out to him.

In the distance, faint, folksy rock music rang out from an acoustic guitar. The notes sounded familiar in a comforting way, though I couldn't name the song.

The closer I got to Nolan's, the louder the music became. When I saw him, sitting on his newly constructed porch strumming his guitar, I also found Gar sitting happily at his feet. Gar barked and Nolan looked up and stopped playing.

"Luring my pets away from me, are you?"

"He just showed up," Nolan said. "Have you decided to keep him?"

"I'm keeping him until someone comes to claim him."

"Oh, right. The posters."

"Hey. When people lose their dog, they stop at nothing to find him. If he belongs to someone, they'll show up." I stepped onto his porch. "What were you playing?"

"Just some old songs. I like folksy stuff."

"Sounded good."

He set the guitar down, to my disappointment, and asked, "What's on the docket for today, counselor?"

I huffed. "More of the same. Hope people show up, keep fixing what's broken, and try to nab a killer."

"I got most of the water out of the pool. Should be ready for a good scrub down."

"Any chance you know something about pool maintenance?"

"I think you put chlorine in it?"

I sighed. "We're going to have to Google pool care and figure it out. Doesn't look like I'll be able to hire someone anytime soon."

"We can manage."

That morning, I worked in my office for a few hours, then headed out to watch Nolan at work. He was filthy and wet, standing in the bottom of the pool, scrubbing the sides with a long-handled scrub brush. Gar bounced around inside the pool's fenced-in area, jumping up and batting at a butterfly before seeing me and bounding over.

"How's it going?" I asked.

Nolan gave a thumb's up. "Want to grab that hose and wash this wall off?"

I picked up the hose and sprayed where he indicated. As I set the hose back down, my finger caught, sending a spray of icy water all over Nolan.

He yelped in surprised and jumped out of the way.

"Sorry! Sorry!"

He glared up at me playfully.

"It was an accident!" I held up my hands in surrender.

He dashed to the steps in the shallow end, and when I realized what he was doing, I snatched up the hose.

He ran at me and I squeezed the nozzle. My spray didn't stop him from gripping me in a bear hug, then turning the water on me. I shrieked and giggled and tried to get away.

He let up and I was able to spray him again, but his arms tightened around me from behind. "Got you now."

"I don't think so."

I thought of the move I'd learned in self-defense class. Drop down while bringing my arms up. But when I tried it, his brute strength kept me from breaking his grasp.

He laughed victoriously and squeezed tighter. I realized I was trapped, and the panic exploded in my chest. Suddenly Russell was holding me again, refusing to let me leave. I gasped a strangled breath and flailed my hands, frantic. "Let go!"

"No way!" He laughed again and flexed his muscles.

"Please," I whimpered, my whole body trembling.

Nolan stopped laughing, and when he released me, I fell to my knees, gasping for air.

He knelt beside me. "Thea? Are you okay? Did I hurt you?"

I covered my face and focused on breathing. *It's okay,* I told myself over and over. *You're safe, and it's okay.* The cold water had soaked me through, making me shiver.

"Can I...?" Nolan asked, worry deep in his voice. "I'm sorry... I'm not sure..."

I couldn't look at him. "Just give me a minute."

He stood back respectfully and waited. When I had calmed enough, I stood and turned to him.

"You didn't hurt me. I just freaked out when I couldn't get away from you."

"Oh." He looked down at his hands. "Sorry. I got carried away. I didn't mean to upset you."

I let out a shaky breath. "I know you didn't. We were just having fun."

"I shouldn't have held you so hard."

His pained expression sparked my guilt and sent a wave of shame through me. "You didn't know. It's okay, really. It's not a big deal. I'll be fine."

He narrowed his eyes at me. "Don't downplay it."

"It's fine."

"It's not. You're obviously upset. I'm here to protect, not harm. I won't fail my unit."

His expression hardened, and the light in his eyes changed. I watched as he seemed to go somewhere else.

"Unit?" I asked. "Nolan?"

He blinked at me a few seconds later. "What?"

"You said something about your 'unit.'"

His brows pulled together in confusion. "Sorry. I meant... here. The campground."

I raised an eyebrow and waited for him to say more. When he didn't, I admitted, "I feel like there's a lot more going on here than either of us is saying."

"Seems that way."

We stared at each other a long while.

"I figure we have two options at this point," he said, finally. "We can sit down and talk it out, if that'll make you feel better. Or we can do what I like to do."

"What's that?"

"Go for a nice long drive and enjoy the country air."

Gar jumped up and barked.

"And of course, Gar can hop in the back," Nolan added. "Whatever you want."

I'd had enough of talking things out in therapy. Nolan didn't need to know all the little details that haunted me. And I felt on edge enough, I didn't need to take a trip down my darkest memory lane. "Let's drive. I need to get out of here for a while."

We changed into dry clothes before piling into his truck and leaving the campground.

"I think better driving," Nolan explained as we cruised down the empty road and past Rollie's.

I lowered the window and closed my eyes, sucking in long breaths of freshness as my hair blew away from my face. The air and its rushing sound soothed me as I watched the trees fly by.

We drove a long time. Eventually, trees became businesses as we reached the closest thing to a downtown that we had in Outer Branson. We passed a doctor's office, and I saw someone familiar.

"Wait! Can you go back?" I asked. "I just saw Marlene walking out of her OB's office."

He pulled into the parking lot, and I had my door open before the truck came to a complete stop. She was several feet from me, approaching a beat-up Chevy sedan.

"Marlene!"

Her head snapped in my direction. "What?"

"I need to know something."

She held a plastic bag labeled "Expectant Mother Care Kit."

"Guess that wasn't a lie," I muttered.

"Excuse me?"

"Why did you have a Cedar Fish Campground map with the overlook circled? What was your part in your sister's death? You can't convince me that you even care she's dead!"

I felt myself losing it, and Nolan's hand on my arm was further proof. I tried to tame my words.

"You don't seem very affected by your twin dying," I said. "And the circled map makes you look guilty, so I think you need to explain."

Marlene puffed up her chest, and I thought she was about to hit me, but instead she burst into tears.

"I wanted her to die, okay?" Marlene whined through her sobs. "You wouldn't understand."

"Try me," I said.

Marlene wiped at her tears, but fresh ones followed. "This is Preston's baby, not Sam's. There is no Sam," she sobbed. "You can't blame me for wanting to be with the father of my child! I begged him to break up with her so he could marry me and we could have a family." She paused to hiccup and suck in fast breaths. "When I got the call that Charlene died, I thought he'd taken it a step further and decided to kill her to be with me. But then that bastard broke up with me the same day!" She bawled for several long minutes.

"So, you think Preston killed Charlene?" I asked.

"He says he didn't."

"What about the map then? And your call to find out which trail had the cliff?"

"Preston took me to the overlook one time when we were meeting up in secret. But I'm afraid of heights, so it made me sick. I threw up and it was so awful that I called to find another trail so I wouldn't puke all over the place again. Jerk thought it was the funniest thing when I got all dizzy. Didn't let me hear the end of it."

"And this is the man you want to be with?" I asked her. "Someone who's mean to you, might have killed your sister, and cheats?"

Her lower lip quivered below her red eyes. "I don't want to raise a baby alone."

"But come on," I insisted. "Do you really want to be Marlene Bean? That's silly. And Preston told me that he was going to propose to Charlene. You don't want to marry a guy like that."

Marlene wailed and put her hands to her face. I glanced back at Nolan and gulped. Probably not a good idea to get a pregnant woman so worked up.

"I really think it's for the best," I said softly. "Preston doesn't seem like someone who will be there for you or your baby."

"He was so mad about Charlene cheating." Marlene sniffled.

"Wait. *Charlene* cheated?"

Marlene nodded. "With Isaac."

"You said he was stalking her."

"She didn't actually cheat, but her and Isaac made it seem like they had messed around in order to piss Preston off."

"I think it worked," I said.

"Preston and Isaac hated each other. Obviously," Marlene said. "And they both loved Charlene."

"Do you think Isaac could have done it?"

"Charlene liked to string him along. Made her feel good to have two men after her. If Charlene was playing games, Isaac might have gotten mad enough. I don't know. She told me she was going to break up with Preston because of the threesome."

"Threesome?" Did I really want more detail on that?

"Preston wanted me and Charlene to have a threesome with him."

I made a disgusted face.

"Exactly," Marlene said. "Charlene was pissed big time. That's why she decided to end it with Preston and start something real with Isaac. She went there that day to tell Isaac. And when Preston found out, he went there to catch them in the act."

"Preston was at the trail that day, too? You've never said that before."

Her eyes widened and she snatched up her bag. "I'm not saying anything! I already talked to the police! Leave me alone!"

Marlene took off running and collided into her car before yanking the door open and getting in. She was barely behind the wheel before she sped off, shooting dust and gravel at us.

"That went well," Nolan said.

"Yeah, I think it did."

He raised an eyebrow. "I was being sarcastic."

"But she gave us a lot of information. And she said Preston was there."

"But you didn't see him on the video," Nolan reminded me.

"Right. Maybe I just missed it."

CHAPTER 14

When Nolan and I returned to Cedar Fish, I had even more on my mind. I still felt frazzled from earlier, and I also felt bad about making Marlene cry. So, when I saw Hennie sitting on her four-wheeler waving at me, I cracked a grateful smile.

"Where you two been off to?" Hennie asked as we climbed out of the truck.

I tapped my leg and Gar jumped out of the back, coming to sit by my side.

"This is the puppy?" Hennie walked over to pet him.

"Yup."

"Nice looking dog. How's Ricky doing?" she asked. "I wanted to check on him and you both. What's the word?"

"Ricky's just fine," Nolan said with a chuckle.

I gave her an apologetic smile. "He kind of... got out. After he tore up the store. Then he snuck in and tore up my cabin."

Hennie whistled. "Guess he was too old to be domesticated."

"I think he's still here in the campground," I said. "Since he got into my cabin last night and all. Keep an eye out."

"Any more on the big case?" Hennie asked.

I shrugged. "A lot of conflicting and confusing information." I recounted our conversation with Marlene. "I don't know that it matters. Doesn't seem like we'll be in business much longer."

"You can't give up without a fight!" Hennie slid one foot back and brought her fists up in a fighting stance. Then she jumped and kicked, crying out, "Hi-yah!" She landed, made a quick swooshing movement with her arms, and then rested back in her fighting stance.

"What was that?" I asked.

"I was just at home, practicing my forms." She did another blocking motion with her arms. "I'm a black belt in Tang Soo Do."

"Oh yeah? Do you think you could teach me some moves?" I glanced sideways at Nolan. I couldn't admit how afraid of him I felt when I thought about our little tussle.

"I think you're better off learning to shoot proper," she said.

"Thea," Nolan accused. "You don't know how to shoot a gun?"

"I do. Kinda."

Hennie tilted her head at me. "Honey, 'kinda' ain't shooting, it's hoping."

"Well then," I said, "can you teach me both?"

"Sure as rain," Hennie said. "In fact, I was just getting ready to go out back and shoot when I get home. Hop on and come along. Nolan can manage here without you."

I looked at him for confirmation, and he said, "Go on. I'll call if I need anything."

I climbed onto the back of the four-wheeler but looked back at Nolan. "Can Gar stay with you? I don't want him running around while we're shooting."

Nolan nodded and rested his hand on the puppy's head.

We cruised along the dirt path back to Hennie's cabin. It looked just as overgrown as last time I'd been there. This time, she took me inside into a large, open room. One corner was a kitchen and another corner led upstairs to a loft that was likely a bedroom. The walls were covered in deer mounts and animal skins. A large fish hung over the fireplace. Inside the fireplace, charred wood gave off the scent of fire.

A black cat dashed across the room, followed by a Husky, then a Maltese, and then a grey-striped cat. They landed in a tumble of meows and barks.

Hennie clapped her hands loudly. "Midnight, Zack, Spook, Tiger!"

The dogs ran to her obediently, while the cats crouched and watched.

"They don't get along too well." She opened the door and the dogs ran out. "That's better. Now we have room. First, I'll teach you a basic karate form."

Hennie performed something that looked like a dance, but with punches and kicks.

"Can you teach me how to get out of holds?"

"Oh sure, we'll get to that."

"Can we skip to that?"

Hennie looked me up and down. "Someone in particular you want to get away from?"

"Anyone who wants to hold me back."

She clapped her hands together. "I gotcha, honey. Let's make this practical. Punch me."

"Uhh..."

"Go on now. Punch me." She tapped her nose. "Right here."

I balled my hand and pushed it into the air toward her face. She stepped out and blocked my punch, then tapped me three times in the stomach with her knuckles.

"We need to work on your punches."

I shook my head. "I really just want defense moves."

Hennie put her hands on her hips. "Now, listen here. I'm not saying you're going to be starting any fights, but offense *is* defense. It's all well and good to get away, but what if you can't?"

I gulped and my moment with Nolan from earlier came back to me.

"Don'tcha want to incapacitate your attacker if you can't break a hold?"

My mind flitted to the memory of Russell's arms tight around me, his hands around my throat, choking me. A flood of emotion followed the memory, bringing tears to my eyes though I managed to push it down in my mind.

I said weakly, "Yes."

Hennie put her hands on my shoulders. "You can do this. Now, here's a good example. If I have you like this, with my hands around your throat, what are you going to do?"

I thought of the move I tried earlier on Nolan. This time, when I dropped down and forced my arms up and out, Hennie's arms flew apart, away from me.

"Perfect," Hennie said.

"What about a bear hug from behind?" I asked.

She nodded. "Tough one if you've got a strong guy to deal with. But lots of options."

She showed me several ways to get free, including things like foot stomps and elbow strikes. I made her practice the moves again and again until I felt like I could do each one well.

"I have to take a break," Hennie said, leaning over with her hands on her knees. "You're wearing me out, lady. I am nearly 60, you know."

The adrenaline pumped through my veins, and I practiced throwing punches and kicks while she rested.

"You ought to get a punching bag," she said. "Build your strength."

"What about shooting? Can we practice that?"

She pulled herself up and took me out back.

"You'll want a handgun for its size, so we'll start there." Hennie handed me a black gun, then showed me how to hold it properly.

I shot several rounds, getting closer to actually hitting the large, round target each time.

"Are you lining up the sights like I showed you?" she asked after I failed again to hit any part of the target.

"I think so." I made the little white dots form a line and then squeezed the trigger. The bullet hit a tree several feet from the target.

"Maybe you're not gripping it tight enough. We'll practice more," Hennie promised as we walked back toward the cabin.

"Are there any moves you can do if someone is trying to push you over a cliff?" I wondered as we stepped inside the large living room again. "Could Charlene have saved herself?"

Hennie thought. "There's always something you can do. Let's see." She walked to the edge of her large bearskin rug and faced away from me. "Try to push me off."

I stood behind her and pushed my palms into her back. She stumbled, but caught herself and turned, grabbing onto me to keep from falling.

"If you had at least one stable foot, you might be able to hurl the other person over and save yourself." She held onto my arm and pulled while twisting around to gain leverage. I tripped forward and stumbled onto the hard wood.

"You're dead," she said.

"Do you think Charlene could have tried to push Preston over, but he stopped her and pushed her instead?"

"He's strong. I would hope that girl isn't stupid enough to try something like that."

"But he could claim self-defense," I pointed out.

"And if he hasn't yet, I'd say it hasn't crossed his mind, which means it didn't happen."

I plopped down on her couch. "This thing is never going to get solved."

"Let's think things through." She wandered into the kitchen and came back with a cardboard tube of cheese balls. "I think better with food."

I dug my hand in and chomped several cheese balls as we talked through the clues again and looked at the crime scene photos on my phone. Without thinking, I wiped my hand on my shirt. "Oh, crap!"

I went to the kitchen sink and first washed the orange off my fingers. I lifted my shirt hem to move it closer to the water but stopped. On my bright blue shirt, the orange cheese smear didn't look orange. It looked brown. Like mud. And my shirt was close to the shade of blue that Preston's hoodie was—the hoodie hanging in his entryway with the brownish-looking smudge.

"Hennie. I think I just solved a murder."

CHAPTER 15

I dashed down the path that connected Hennie's cabin to the campground, eager to find Nolan. I texted as I hurried, "Where are you?"

He responded, "Pool."

I headed straight there and found him painting the pool's walls. Gar jumped up when he saw me and ran over, jumping up to lick my face—which wasn't much of a jump for the huge puppy.

"Hi boy." I rubbed his head and patted his back.

"You learn how to wax a car?" Nolan asked.

"Not exactly, but I learned more ways to get out of that hold you had me in earlier."

He squinted up at me. "I'll never do that again."

"No, you should. We should practice."

"I don't think that's a good idea. Anyway, I'm covered in paint."

"It's looking good so far. That's a nice shade of blue."

He dipped the brush in and added more paint to the wall.

"Hey, so, I solved the murder today," I said casually, inspecting my nails.

He chuckled. "You think so? How's that now?"

"When I was at Hennie's, I got cheese ball cheese on my shirt and it looked the same as the smudge on Preston's hoodie. And when Hennie and I did a reenactment of what might have happened when Charlene fell, I think the smudges are consistent with her reaching out to grab him as she went over."

He pulled his eyebrows together in thought. "You could have something there. That could tie him to the scene, except there's nothing to tie that hoodie to the scene. Unless there's fiber evidence, but I don't recall anything in the database."

"Eyewitness. Isaac said he saw Preston on the trail. I thought he was lying to make himself look innocent, but what if he wasn't?"

He shook his head. "But we didn't see Preston on the video, even when we went back through it, and with no evidence of an alternate path to the trail..."

"I know. But it had to be him. Nothing else fits."

"Without solid evidence, it won't matter."

I sighed. "Well, what can I do?"

"I'd write everything down. Reason out why you think Preston did it. We can go to the police tomorrow and talk to them. Maybe you'll give them new information that will help."

That evening, I did as Nolan suggested. Sitting on my porch, watching Gar dart around in all his puppy energy, I laid out my entire statement as if I had been a criminal defense lawyer and was going to be giving a closing argument. When I was done, I felt confident that I had done well and proved my case. Now, I just had to get the cops to believe it so they could find solid evidence to lock Preston away.

I went to bed with renewed hope. If the murder could be wrapped up, things could return to normal, and the campground would be saved. The stress in my chest loosened, and I fell into the best sleep I'd had in a long time. Unfortunately, it didn't last.

Gar's growling woke me suddenly. I lay in bed, frozen, listening. Then I heard a loud thump downstairs.

I quietly slid out of bed and grabbed my gun from my bedside table. *Thank you, Hennie,* I thought as I pulled back the slide to load the chamber. If she hadn't insisted that I borrow her gun and keep it loaded and close by, I wouldn't have taken it out of my safe—it would be locked in my bedroom closet while the key was downstairs in my purse.

Gar pressed himself against me, his hair standing up, and we moved together to the door. I thought to call Nolan, but my clock said 3:13, and I didn't want to wake him if it was nothing more than Ricky breaking in again. I stuck my phone in my pocket just in case.

The bedroom door hadn't been closed all the way—something I might reconsider in the future—so I pushed it open and slipped out onto the landing at the top of the stairs. Gar moved like a fuzzy ninja at my side, a constant low rumbling growl in his chest.

A shadow moved in the living room. The railing blocked my view, but I was sure it wasn't a usual shadow. It looked like the shape of a person sitting on the sofa.

As I held my breath and watched, the shadow moved again. A page in my notebook turned.

"Freeze!" I aimed the gun and stepped sideways down the stairs, Gar trailing after me.

The shadow jumped up, and when I reached the bottom of the stairs, the moonlight illuminated Preston's face.

He laughed. "Do you think you're going to shoot me?"

"I hope I won't have to. I'm going to call the police. I know you killed Charlene, and I'm going to prove it."

He shook his head. "You know Thea, I thought my little note would stop you from interfering. I thought you were smarter than this, but Marlene tells me you just won't give up." He waved my notebook at me before tearing it in half. "You leave me no choice."

He threw himself at me and reached out to grab the gun. Gar barked and grabbed Preston's shirt in his teeth, pulling as he growled.

Hennie and I had practiced what to do if someone tried to disarm me. But as I tried to break his hold on my hand, my foot slipped. I crashed hard to the ground.

Preston took a moment to recover and position the gun in his hand. In that moment of distraction, I launched a kick to his groin as Gar leapt on him. Preston grunted and stepped back but recovered quickly and aimed the gun at my head.

Hennie's instructions came back to me: *If you can't get them down, get yourself away.* I bolted forward and yanked open the front door. Gar's heavy footfalls and panting followed me. I dared to look back and saw Preston not far behind.

My body wasn't used to sprinting. My chest heaved and burned. My legs didn't want to move, but the terror pushed me forward.

A gun shot rang into the air, cracking the stillness of the night. In the same instant, a tree just feet from my head splintered as the bullet hit it. Gar yelped and cowered in fear until I called to him.

A few feet ahead, I saw a small break in the trees. I turned suddenly, hoping Preston wouldn't see, and bolted down the unmarked trail. Tree roots and rocks littered the path. Pain stabbed my ankle as it twisted on a rock, but I kept moving.

The darkness didn't help me avoid obstacles, and now that I was in thicker trees, the moonlight was mostly obstructed. I ran with my hands in front of me to block the branches that reached out to grab me. Gar kept up, but the brush had slowed his pace as well.

A small clearing became visible, and I turned a sharp right to join the bigger path. I kept running and realized I was on the west trail. The trail I'd just exited was not one marked on any map I'd ever seen and wasn't maintained by the campground. But, since the west trail ran so close to the north trail in that section, and the ground was all gravel, it provided a way onto the north trail that didn't involve using the entrance or exit or traipsing through brush, leaving behind a visible path. And the police hadn't bothered to search the other trails for smaller side trails.

In my distraction, I missed a branch and felt a sharp sting as it whacked my eye. I stumbled, pressing my fingers to my eye as it watered and burned. Something hard thumped my back. My knees gave out and I smacked the ground.

Preston was on top of me, pinning me with his weight as I struggled to move. My panic blanked my mind and I could do nothing but swat at him and flinch away.

He got his hands around my throat, pressing my face into the ground, and suddenly I was back on the kitchen floor of my duplex and my ex-husband was on top of me. My stomach churned. I knew what would come next.

"No, Russell! Don't do this! Not again!" I screamed.

Gar bit his side and Preston's scream brought me back to the present. His weight eased some, and I flipped over in time to see him punch Gar's nose. Gar yelped and backed off. Preston tightened his grip on my throat, and my air lessened.

"This is so much more satisfying," Preston said. "I should have done this to Charlene instead of pushing her over the cliff. And maybe that punk, Isaac. I shouldn't have let him walk away after I beat him."

I barely heard Preston's words as I tried to throw him off me using one of the hip-thrust moves I learned from Hennie, but he weighed too much. With both of his hands around my throat, however, that meant mine were free.

I brought my right arm up and over, colliding into Preston's forearms. His grip loosened, but he regained it quickly.

I felt something hard pressing into my hip and realized it was my gun in Preston's jeans. I reached down and closed my fingers on it. Preston let go with one hand, trying to stop me from taking the gun while still strangling me.

I couldn't get the gun free from his waistband, but as I tugged on it, I felt the trigger slip into place under my finger. I pressed it against Preston and pulled.

The shot made my ears ring. Preston hollered in pain as he lay on his side. He gripped his thigh, where blood poured from a fresh wound.

Gar had Preston's ankle in his teeth like a steel trap. I scrambled to my feet, aimed the gun at Preston's head, and loaded another bullet in the chamber.

"I should just shoot you." Part of me wanted to pull the trigger badly, to see someone who would commit such violence be gone from this earth forever. But I didn't need someone's death on me, even if he deserved it.

I reached for my phone and saw that my screen had been cracked. Fresh panic slid over me as I tried to swipe to unlock the screen. With my hand shaking and sweating, still holding the gun and doing my best not to lose it, I couldn't get the phone unlocked to make a call. All I could manage was holding down the button until I heard the little voice-command chime.

I said, "Call Nolan," and my phone dialed.

He answered with, "Where are you? Are you okay? I heard gunshots."

"North trail. Near the pond. I shot Preston in the leg. After he confessed to killing Charlene."

"I'm on my way."

After five minutes, Gar's ears twisted, and he looked down the trail. He didn't let go of Preston's ankle, though Preston had stopped trying to kick free. A moment later, Nolan ran into sight.

He wore a t-shirt and jersey shorts and had broken into a sweat, but he looked like an absolute angel. When I saw him, my whole body sank inches in relief. Tears filled my eyes, and I had to focus to keep the gun trained on Preston.

Nolan yanked Preston's arm to flip him over and pushed his knee into Preston's back. He pulled out shiny handcuffs and closed them around Preston's wrists. Nolan stood, then pulled Preston to his feet by his hands. Preston cried out in pain and Nolan kneed him in the back to move him forward. Preston limped one step and fell.

"Get up, you worthless piece of crap." Nolan kicked Preston's butt hard enough that he ate dirt.

"I don't think he can walk," I said.

"I don't care," Nolan snapped. "I'm not going to let some lowlife get away with murder! Not again."

His words smacked me. *Not again.* It was the same thing I'd said when I flashed back to the last time Russell attacked me.

I stepped forward and put my hand on Nolan's arm like he'd done to me when I'd been out of line with Marlene. He refused to turn toward me. That same distant look I'd seen before was in his eyes. It took a moment for his stony expression to soften.

My heart ached for him. Whatever was going on his mind clearly troubled him like my past haunted me. "It's okay," I said. "Whatever happened before, it's not happening again."

He took a slow breath and nodded once. "The police will be here soon," he said. "And then this will all be over."

CHAPTER 16

Two weeks after the night Preston attacked me, my alarm went off early. I tapped my phone and hopped out of bed, heart already pumped with excitement.

Gar sat on alert, awaiting my command. He scratched at his new collar—a reflective neon yellow so I could find him in the woods easily and so cars could see him.

"Today's the big day," I told him. "Aren't you excited?"

He tilted his head. I couldn't blame him. I felt nervous myself. I'd dared to spend a small chunk of the estate money on this event, in hopes it would bring in fresh business and positive press for the campground. But I'd never planned something like this and felt unsure about most of my decisions.

"Come on!" I dashed downstairs and he bounded after me, yipping playfully. I gave him a treat before we headed out the door.

When we reached the rec room, I poured my premium grounds into the coffee machine before starting it. I'd promised top-notch coffee as part of my bribe to my helpers. As if the scent alone had called to them, Nolan and Hennie arrived just as the coffee finished brewing.

I poured and they drank. The three of us sipped and yawned as the caffeine made its way through our bodies.

"Need about four more of these." Hennie gulped from her mug, then set it down. "Whose idea was it to get up so early?"

"We have a lot to do," I explained. "These balloons aren't going to fill themselves."

Nolan picked up a red balloon and filled it from the helium tank, then sucked the air out and said, in a high-pitched helium-laden voice, "Yes, ma'am."

By the time the morning faded to noon, we'd blown up all the balloons and scattered them across various amenities that we wanted to draw attention to: the office, rec hall, pool, playground, mini-golf course, wildlife pen, and horseshoe pits. A large banner hung below the Cedar Fish sign at the entrance proclaiming, "Grand Reopening! Memorial Day Cookout - 4 p.m. to 10 p.m."

Tiki torches lined the main paths, waiting for their time to shine. Glittery spinners and crepe paper embellished the large pavilion, where the food would be served. A table to one side, surrounded by signs and balloons, advertised pricing and made it as easy as possible to make a reservation. New tubes and balls floated in the clear water of the pool, and I'd even tied patriotic ribbons around necks of the few animals I managed to catch in the wildlife pen.

I went to check on Curtis while Hennie cleaned up our pizza boxes from lunch and Nolan prepared the bonfire. When I entered the office, Curtis sat up sharply on his stool and looked around.

"Don't let me wake you," I muttered.

I cleared off the counter and answered the phone when it rang.

"Is this the campground where the murder took place?" a woman asked.

"Unfortunately, yes, it is." I held my breath.

In the background, the woman shouted, "Verne! I've got it! Do you want to stay five or six nights?" Then back to me, "Do you all have weekly rates?"

In my shock, I stuttered, "Y-yes actually." I ran through the nightly and weekly rates and booked two sites, side-by-side, for one week in August.

"Do you have any questions?" I asked as I entered her reservation in the logbook.

"Yes," the woman said. "Will the couple who stopped the murderer be there? We want to have them autograph our newspaper."

"Well... yeah. That's me, actually, and our security guard." I chuckled.

"Oh!" Again to Verne, "I'm talking to her *right now*!" She returned. "How exciting! We just can't wait to come and see in person where that poor girl was killed and you took down her killer."

"We look forward to having you." *I think.* I hung up with a strange expression on my face as Nolan walked in.

"Something wrong?"

"I just booked two weeks' worth of sites because they want to come and meet the famous couple who stopped a murderer and see where it all took place."

He whistled. "Oh, boy. I didn't sign on for fame."

"Me either, but if we can use that to get reservations, I don't have a problem signing a few autographs, do you?"

"Not when you put it like that."

"Think of it as job security. Though, we'll have to make it clear that we're not a couple and I'm your boss."

He pulled his mouth into a half smile. "Of course."

I looked up as the door jingled. A family walked in and looked around. A minute later, a couple walked in.

"I guess people are arriving already." My watch said 2:18. "If a lot more people come, let's start the food early."

"I'm off to my post."

Nolan's main duty for the day, besides grilling tons of hot dogs, was to watch for any possible mischief. We discussed the possibility that there could be backlash. A friend of Preston's who wasn't happy about him serving jail time. Or maybe Marlene would show up and decide that I had ruined her life and stolen her baby's daddy from her. We were prepared for anything from bee stings to a gunfight.

Hennie would serve as undercover backup security, but her main focus was to oversee the food and answer questions. Curtis would man the cash register in the store and office, as always, and I would float around, taking reservations—hopefully—answering questions, and apparently, signing autographs.

Gar matched the staff in his new dark-green t-shirt with the Cedar Fish logo front and center in white lettering. His only job was to look cute and draw in families. I'd put him on dropped-food-clean-up duty later. I did have a slight worry that someone would try to claim him, but after I'd taken him to the vet for a checkup and had a tracking chip put in, I felt like he'd become officially mine. The tag on his collar even said so. I'd taken down the few "Lost Dog" flyers I'd put up.

When Nolan messaged that he thought it was time to start the food, I went to the rec hall to check my special creation. I pierced one meatball with a fork and held it out toward Nolan. "Moment of truth."

He took a bite and closed his eyes as a slow smile spread across his face.

"Yeah?" I asked.

He put his hand on his stomach. "Oh, yeah."

I popped one of the keftedakia into my mouth. "Perfection."

Nolan nodded. His cheeks bulged with meat as he stuffed one more ball in before stopping to chew.

"These are supposed to be for the guests," I said.

He took a while to chew, made a huge swallow, and claimed, "I just wanted to make sure they were okay first."

I gave him a half smile. "I guess it's true what they say about the way to a man's heart."

He stuffed two more meatballs in his mouth and rubbed his stomach. "Works every time."

Things picked up quickly then. Over the next hours, people poured in—more than I imagined would come. More than we had room to park. Nolan had improvised and roped off a section of the lawn to become overflow parking. The hot dogs ran out in the evening, and I called Enid, begging her to make an emergency delivery.

When I saw Enid tottering toward the pavilion in a bright-red sweater covered in white and blue crocheted stars, I got up to meet her.

"So good to see you!" I gave her a quick hug. "I thought you'd send Arlo. Since you're here, you've got to taste my keftedakia."

"I did bring Arlo."

Enid pointed to him carrying a large box of hot dogs toward Nolan.

"Thank you so much for that. I thought we had more than enough."

"Best sort of problem to have. This place is starting to look good."

"You think so?"

I gazed out over the grounds. The sun hung low in the late afternoon sky. Kids splashed in the pool and climbed

on the jungle gym. Adults stood in groups talking, playing cornhole or horseshoes, watching their kids chase
each other in groups of twos and threes. I'd taken multiple reservations, and when Nolan had done a ride through
of the campground, he reported that people were fishing
and wading in the water at the swimming beach. A make-
shift memorial had sprung up in front of the new railing
and around the small, wooden cross we'd installed to mark
Charlene's place of death. We had several walk-ins for that
night and the upcoming week.

Enid put her arm around my shoulders. "I knew you
could do it. You're exactly what this place needs."

"See if you still think so highly of me after you taste my
keftedakia."

I scooped several meatballs into a bowl with the sauce
and handed it to her. She took a careful bite and her eyes
widened. "Nostima!"

"I added some red wine vinegar," I confessed. "It
seemed like it needed it."

"Red wine vinegar..." She took on a thoughtful stare,
then asked, "Didn't I tell you to put that in?"

I shook my head.

She laughed. "I'd forget my head... You must have
Greek blood."

I chuckled. "That's high praise, but I don't. I'm Italian."

She quirked an eyebrow. "You sure about that?"

"Pagoni? Definitely Italian."

She shrugged. "Well then, you'll have to make some Italian meatballs and share the recipe."

"Only problem is, I hate Italian food. Weird, huh?"

Enid shrugged again. "We're all special in our own way."

"Excuse me," a man said as he approached. "Are you the owner?"

"Yes, I am."

He stuck his hand out. "Gary Simpson, president of the Spook Stalkers. We have a yearly convention, and each year, we find a haunted venue to add to the fun. We like to go on ghost hunts, and places where violence occurred have some of the best chances of getting action. We're wondering if Cedar Fish Campground might be our venue for next year's convention."

My eyes widened. "How much space would you need?"

"We expect about two hundred adults. And the use of something like that building." He gestured to the rec hall.

"If most of you will be camping, we can certainly accommodate."

"Fabulous. Can I book it now? I'd like to have the information available before this year's convention."

"Certainly."

When I'd finished taking down his information and he walked away, a woman approached me with a timid demeanor. I'd had enough people ask for an autograph that I wasn't shocked by her apologetic smile.

"Hi, you're Thea?" she asked.

I stuck out my hand, and she flinched, then placed her hand in mine and shook it.

"I'm Sally Becker? You said to stop by and introduce myself if I had a chance?"

"Oh right!" I stood and gestured for her to follow me. "I'm glad you could make it. I also have the application, which we'll need to have on file, so you can take that with you and bring it Tuesday when you start."

After I got her the application, I introduced her to Curtis. "This is your summer help," I said loudly. "Sally will be answering phones, taking reservations, and ringing up campers."

He squinted at Sally and slowly put out his hand. She daintily shook it.

We said hello to Hennie outside, then found Nolan by the grill.

"That's our tiny crew," I explained to Sally. "And Hennie doesn't technically work here. Did you bring your family?"

Sally pointed to where two young boys took turns beating each other with plastic buckets. She gave me a grimacing smile. "They're twins." She forced a chuckle as one wailed loudly. "Boys, right?" Her breathing picked up and she glanced at me again. "Is there any alcohol available for purchase?" Her eyes begged me to say yes.

"Sorry. We don't have a license for that sort of thing."

She nodded and balled her small hands into fists. "It'll be fine." She charged over to the boys and bravely stepped into the brawl to tear them apart.

"Ouch," I said as one of the boys whacked her with the bucket.

"She doesn't look like she can handle much," Nolan said.

"As long as she can handle the phones and campers, that's all that matters. I don't know what else to do. I can't bear to fire Curtis, even if he sleeps most of the day and can barely do the job, no one else answered the ad, and we need at least one more person for the summer."

"Just glad that we have enough coming in to fund another employee."

"Yeah." I rubbed the black hair between Gar's ears. "It's not too bad, is it, Gar-Gar? Maybe this won't turn out to be a disaster after all."

Nolan jerked his head toward the empty hot dog boxes. "Judging by how many hot dogs we went through, I'd say we did pretty good. We take in some reservations?"

"Tons. And we even have a Spook Stalkers convention next summer."

"What's that?"

"Ghost hunters."

"Hunters? Do they... try to fight ghosts?"

I shrugged. "I think it's more about making contact? Do you think Charlene's ghost is walking around?"

"Her murderer is facing jail for life. I'd say she's found her justice and moved on."

"I hope so." I shivered to think of ghosts wandering the grounds at night.

"Not all spirits are bad. Don't you feel your grandparents here?"

I smiled, picturing Grandad pushing me on the swings. "They're everywhere I look. This place has a lifetime of memories. My first kiss happened right there." I pointed to the last picnic table under the pavilion. "The summer I was fourteen, I had a crush on a camper, and on his last night, Tommy Parks planted a wet one right on my lips."

"Very romantic." Nolan smirked.

I shoved him lightly. "Was your first kiss any better?"

He formed a smug grin. "Top of the Ferris wheel, on her birthday, after I gave her a charm bracelet."

I was surprised to feel a flicker of envy at this revelation. "Well, aren't you the romantic one?" I teased.

"Not everybody thinks so." He rubbed his stomach. "Any of that keftedakia left?"

"Long gone. Sorry."

"Damn. I'm starving."

"I've seen you eat no fewer than five hot dogs. That's not counting all the pizza, chips, meatballs, pretzels, and ice cream cups you also ate."

He gave me a defensive huff. "I thought you understood the importance of quality assurance."

I laughed. "Consider it part of your salary."

"In that case..." He set three more hot dogs on the grill.

Hennie walked over to us, a lighter in hand. "All set, boss."

All of the tiki torches had been lit and the strands of lights turned on. The place hummed with life and energy. I watched a man toss a horseshoe with his adult son and saw my grandad and dad taking turns. Kids laughed and ran around the playground, just like my cousins and I used to. Over at the pool, a girl and her grandmother reminded me of my first swimming lesson and how my sister wouldn't stop splashing me while Grandma tried to convince me to let go of the wall. My mom and sister and I had spent hours at the now-packed mini-golf course, perfecting our swings so that one of us could beat Grandad—which we never had.

So many great old memories, and this moment was one of my favorite new memories. The presence of Grandma and Grandad surrounded me. They had spent half of their life there, and all of mine. It was the only place I could picture them, though they had come to visit us in the city many times.

Nolan stood beside me, hands on his hips, gazing out at the crowd with me. "Looks like a success."

Everywhere I turned, I saw happy people taking advantage of all my grandparents had built. Even old Dill was curled up in the lap of an older woman who petted her while swinging lazily on the porch swing just outside the office.

I smiled. "Yeah, I think we pulled it off."

I hoped my grandparents were up in heaven, looking down on me. And I hoped they felt proud of what they saw.

Find out more about how Gar came to Cedar Fish Campground in the short story "Fishy Beginnings."

When Gar's secret past is discovered, Thea must fight to keep her beloved pet.

Gar, a black Newfoundland puppy, mysteriously showed up at Cedar Fish Campground and became the perfect companion to heal Thea's grief-stricken, dog-loving heart. With such a serendipitous beginning, Thea never questioned the life Gar had before he found her. But one newspaper article could change everything.

Thea discovers a secret about Gar that could mean she loses him forever. With help from her ex-cop security guard, Nolan, and her quirky sidekick, Hennie, Thea must draw on her past to win the right to keep Gar before she loses another treasured pet.

FISHY BEGINNINGS is a short story that takes place after the events of *Between a Rock and a Deadly Place*, book one in the Cedar Fish Campground Series. If you love dogs or have ever lost a pet, you'll love this tale of hilarious animal antics and moments that will both break and warm your pet-loving heart.

Get the story FREE
when you join my mailing list!

ZoeyChase.com/FishyBeginnings

Acknowledgments

The problem with book acknowledgments is that so much more goes into every book than what is seen on the page. It takes years of perfecting a craft, a lot of encouragement and critique, and tons of red ink. I'll focus on this book alone for the sake of space, because if I listed everyone who's helped me in my writing journey, you'd have another book to read. If you're one of those people, you know who you are. Thank you.

God, who made me a writer and gave me the words and desire to start this calling and who is the core of everything.

Always, Jonathan, you are the one who helps me keep things moving. To my girls and family, thank you for listening and caring and helping me name things.

My beta readers, who made sure this book didn't suck: Claire, Janet, Alan, Angela.

My critique partners, who have helped improve my writing tremendously over the years: Doogie, Eileen, Janet, Jon, Madhu, Mary Alice, Peter, Susan.

My awesome editor, Annie, who found all the holes and weak spots.

Kristin, who kept me motivated and sane.

Mark Dawson and the SPF 101 community, who made me believe I could succeed and guided the way.

And to you, dear reader, for taking the time to visit Cedar Fish Campground and hang out with me. See you again soon!

Note from the Author

Thank you so much for reading BETWEEN A ROCK AND A DEADLY PLACE. I hope you enjoyed your time with Thea and her crew. I had a blast writing it, and I can't wait to get back there!

Would you consider leaving a review?

Reviews are a huge help to indie authors like me. I'd be grateful if you would give just a few minutes of your time to let others know what you thought of the book. Reviews not only help other readers find the books they're looking for, they help indie authors get seen.

Leave a review:
ZoeyChase.com/BetweenARockAndADeadlyPlace

Thank you!
Zoey Chase

Don't miss the next book in the series!

The Regional Cornhole Semi-Finals are all fun and games... until the head official is ruled dead.

Thea Pagoni has her hands full trying to please the very particular Hugo Menendez, head official of the Regional Cornhole Semi-Finals. After the bad press from a recent murder at the campground, Thea is counting on this event to turn things around. When security guard/ handyman Nolan finds Hugo dead—then finds himself named the prime suspect—Thea doesn't know what to believe. The campground cat falls ill, and Thea turns to her loyal friend, Hennie, to help her sort out the truth and make a tough decision about an employee.

With a campground full of potential suspects, witnesses, and evidence, Thea scrambles to find something that will clear Nolan and bring justice for Hugo. She must decipher the murderer's clues, while still managing the event and all of its participants, before Nolan is arrested and the campground suffers more bad press and cancellations.

Get it here:
ZoeyChase.com/BreathOfFatalAir

Read the first chapter of

BREATH OF FATAL AIR

now in this special preview!

To find out more or to purchase, visit:

ZoeyChase.com/BreathOfFatalAir

A rumble crept into the stillness of the early morning quiet. A loud muffler. The car making the racket appeared out of the wisps of fog blanketing the road. Gar, my Newfoundland puppy, lifted his head, and I reached down from my seat on the campground's office porch swing to pet him. "This should be interesting," I muttered.

An old silver Dodge Dart, painted with a thick, checkered wave along its body, pulled into the campground entrance. At the back of the car, a bright red and a bright blue corn bag were featured as the dominant art. The front of the car boasted two flags, one on each side like a government official's car, displaying the red, blue, and white logo of the Worldwide Cornhole Organization—the WCO.

Rather than turn into the parking lot, the car stopped in the entrance road, just past the large sign that read "Cedar Fish Campground." A man in a long-sleeved button-down shirt and sharp pants approached. His tie boasted an image of a cornhole platform and bean bag. I stood and Gar got to his feet beside me.

I got a good view of the man's face and froze in shock. A photo jumped into my mind. Grandad, in his late thirties like I was now, sitting on a picnic table, smiling like he was holding back a secret. When I saw the man approaching, it was like that captured image of Grandad had walked out of the photo. I couldn't shake the eerie feeling, and it made my knees wobbly.

"Hello there, fine woman." The man dipped his head and held out a hand to me, palm up. "Hugo Menendez. Who might you be, divine creature?"

I had to remember that this was more than a camper. Hugo was responsible for bringing a huge event to my campground—business I very much wanted to repeat year after year. But he was particular. He'd been hard to work with in the weeks of planning, so I needed to make sure every detail of the event was flawless. That pressure, combined with the bizarre hollow, haunted feeling, made me shaky and scattered.

I blinked at him, then put my hand in his. "Thea Pagoni."

"Exactly who I was looking for and hoped you'd be. That is my vehicle there." He turned to point, as if there were any question. "I don't see your preferred parking, however. Or a valet?"

"Oh, we don't..." I looked around, frantic. Had there been a request for that? Had we missed something?

"No trouble. I'll just leave it there until you've got me checked in."

"We'll get it taken care of right away." I turned and entered the office with Gar.

Hugo was right on my heels and leaned on the counter as I looked up his reservation. "Must be nice living in a place like this," he said. "Quiet and peaceful. You look quite healthy and well rested."

I wasn't sure what to think of the compliment or his tone. Was he... flirting? "Thanks. It's been mostly good."

Hugo pulled a thick book from his messenger bag. "This is the rule book we'll need to go over to make sure everything is up to regulation."

"I've had my handyman working on the things you mentioned in your email."

"Working on?" Hugo straightened up and looked around. "Surely, things are completed and ready for the competition, are they not?"

I gulped. Crap. Were we behind schedule? "Oh, yeah. I just meant... He wants to show you the field and make sure it's all right."

"*Field?* Darling, it's called a *court*." Hugo flipped the book open. "Now, I sent very specific schematics for how the court is to be set up. Surely, your man has read it?"

"Yeah, he..."

I recalled handing the thick book to Nolan, my security guard and campground handyman, shortly after we'd booked the Regional Cornhole Semi-Final Competition. He'd glanced at it, but said he knew how to make a cornhole field. I had trusted him. I'd figured that we had the wooden boxes and corn bags, so what else was there? But now, looking at Hugo's frantic turning of pages, it was clear we'd missed it.

I picked up my new walkie talkie and pressed the button to call Nolan. "Hey, I need you in the office. The cornhole official is here."

"10-4."

I smiled at Hugo. "He's on his way."

Hennie, my friend, sidekick, and honey provider, burst through the door in her muddy galoshes, carrying a large box of various honey products. Her long, silver braid looked frizzy and wild today from the humidity in the June air. "Hey, some jackass is blocking your entrance."

I pressed my lips into a line and widened my eyes at her while nodding subtly toward Hugo.

Hennie set the box down and gave Gar's head a tussle before saying to Hugo, "Well, there. I shoulda guessed that was your car based on all the cornholing." She pointed to his tie.

Hugo turned to raise an eyebrow at her. "And you are?"

Hennie stuck out a hand. "Henrietta Schrute. Proud cornhole fan for a lifetime."

Hugo turned back to me with a smirk. "So glad that some of our fans are as lovely as you."

My cheeks warmed, and I glanced at Hennie, who rocked back on her heels.

I gave her an awkward, sympathetic smile. "Thanks for bringing the order," I said. "You know where to put it."

Nolan stepped into the office. Gar bolted to him, tail wagging so hard that it shook his body. Nolan petted Gar and took Hugo in before approaching.

"Hey there. Nolan Cade." Nolan stuck his hand out and shook Hugo's, hard. "Want to take a look at things?"

"He needs to get to his site first," I said. "So his car isn't in the way."

Hugo waved me off. "It can sit there a while. I need to make sure the courts have been properly designed. It sounds like things have not been up to par around here, and it's very distressing."

Nolan blew out a breath and looked at me.

I gave them both a nervous, apologetic smile. "I'm sure that Nolan will have everything exactly as it needs to be."

Hugo pulled his mouth into another charming grin. "If you tell him what to do, I have no doubt, darling."

I gulped and dared to look at Nolan. His face slid into a glare that mirrored Hennie's. Hugo pushed his way out the door, calling behind him, "Come now, Mr. Cade. Let's get things going as they should be."

Nolan growled in his throat before following Hugo.

"Now, there's a real piece of work," Hennie said.

"Yeah," I agreed, but my stomach tightened. We had to make sure Hugo was happy if this event was going to go well. The way he looked so much like Grandad warmed me to him in a way that played against the repulsion I felt at his smarminess and demanding attitude. Just being in his presence felt like a tug of war on my soul, not helped by the way he'd been over-flattering toward me.

A moment later, my walkie crackled. "Get out here," Nolan said.

Hennie and I hurried out the door, Gar at our feet, as Curtis, my much older employee, shuffled toward us.

"Hey, Curtis." I waved.

He jerked a thumb at the entrance, where his old Buick now sat behind Hugo's Dodge. "Ran out to get milk. Can't get back in."

I said back into the walkie, "We need to get Hugo's car out of the entry."

"*Get over here,*" Nolan responded.

Our shoes made squeaking sounds in the wet grass as Hennie and I hurried to the field we'd designated to be the cornhole *court*. We'd had a lot of rain recently, which had softened the ground. I worried it would cause problems. At the court, Hugo's hands were in the air, and he waved his rule book at Nolan.

"Oh, boy," Hennie said, staying close to my side. "This'll be good."

Nolan ran his hand through his dark hair and scowled at me.

"Nothing here meets regulation," Hugo announced. "This is a disaster! My entire career is on the line, you know!"

"Your... career as a cornhole official?" Nolan asked.

Hugo put his hands on his hips. "In two days, we will have twenty-three contestants and hundreds of spectators here for this competition. If it's not perfect, you will hear from my lawyers."

I jumped on that one. "You've already heard from ours." I forced a chuckle. "I happen to be a corporate lawyer." Hopefully that would keep him from making lawsuit threats.

Hugo tilted his head toward me. "Don't you just get better by the minute."

My face flushed and I looked down. Not the response I'd wanted. "It was another life."

"You've got to tell me more about it sometime," Hugo said.

"I hate to break up this little... whatever"—Nolan flicked his hand in the air—"but if we have so much to do, let's get on with it already."

"The courts need to be reconfigured immediately to fix the dimensions." Hugo turned, pointed his nose in the air, and stormed off.

"Where did you find this guy?" Nolan asked me.

I lifted one shoulder and Nolan huffed in response before charging off after Hugo.

I asked Hennie, "Any chance you can help Nolan today?"

She nodded and followed the men.

Another voice called out from the front of the campground, and I looked over to see a chubby man in dress pants and a bright-orange satin shirt hurrying for us, flittering his hands frantically. "Hello! Hello! Help!"

I walked over to meet him. "What can I do for you?"

"There's some sort of backup." He waved toward the campground entrance, where three cars now filled the short space before the gate. "I'm Ray Kline, assistant official. I need to be checked in immediately and taken to my cabin. Hugo Menendez is expecting me."

"You go on then." I pointed in Hugo's direction. "I wouldn't keep him waiting if I were you."

"Oh no, certainly not." Ray hurried off, stepping daintily over the grass.

I went into the office to get Ray's cabin key and check-in form. I'd have to get him to complete it later. I walked outside to inspect the line of cars. Sally, my final employee to arrive at work, sat in her white minivan in the main road, her turn signal on, waiting to turn in. She must not have noticed that no one sat in the three cars ahead of her in line.

Luckily, Hugo had left his keys in his car. For the valet, of course. I hopped in and parked his car in the office lot. I retrieved Curtis's keys from him, then moved his and Ray's cars as well. Sally turned in behind me and rushed out of her van.

"I am *so* sorry I'm late. I don't know what the holdup was there."

"They left their cars in the entrance," I explained. "Don't worry about it."

She blinked at me in confusion.

"The officials are already here, and Nolan and Hennie are trying to get things set up. I'll be in to help you at the desk as much as I can. It'll be busy today."

Sally nodded confidently. She took out a small glass vial. "I brought my lavender essential oil, so I'll be nice and calm all day." She grinned and tucked the oil back into her pocket.

Too bad she didn't have her oil last week, when she encountered an older camper who wasn't unhappy, but had a lot of questions and took a lot of time. Sally had been tired and frazzled that morning—her twin boys had had her up late, fighting over who got to sleep with the special blanket. The woman camper had been surprised at Sally's angry outburst, but hadn't held a grudge when I took her aside to explain. The woman must've been a mom, too.

I left Sally in the office, sniffing her oil, and Gar and I returned to the scene at the cornhole court. Nolan and Hennie held stakes and a thin rope while Hugo and Ray held measuring tapes and barked orders over one another.

"Anything I can do to help?" I asked.

Hugo came over to me with an armful of corn bags. "None of these are regulation. I will have to tap into my personal equipment. We'll never get WCO approved bags in time. I cannot believe this—is happening."

"There are regulation corn bags?" I asked.

"Well, of course," Ray snapped.

Gar gave a warning rumble from his chest and pressed his body against me in defense.

"How dare you speak to a woman like that?" Hugo said to Ray. Then to me, "Darling, I know you don't understand the rules of cornhole—it is a rather complicated sport, after all. I'd love to sit down over dinner and explain all the regulations I'm responsible for." He adjusted his armload of corn bags and pulled his mouth into a sneering smile.

I had to look away. When he talked to me like that and looked at me like that—while he resembled my grandad so much—it made my skin crawl.

"Let's get these courts set before you worry about your dinner plans," Nolan said.

Hugo wiggled his eyebrows at me. "It would be my honor to spend the evening with you rather than this imbecile." He jerked a thumb at Ray. "I'm sure you can understand my preference."

I didn't know how to respond. If I turned him down, it might upset him and make him even more difficult to deal with, which would be bad for everyone. But going out with him would be very bad for me. I caught Nolan's disgusted glare and decided to be safe and sidestep. "What's the problem with the courts, exactly?"

"The pitcher boxes are the wrong sizes and the foul lines are off," Nolan snapped. "And the platforms aren't made of thick enough wood and don't have the right paint."

I sucked in a breath. "Give me a list and I'll get whatever we need."

Nolan scribbled down a list of items, then thrust the paper at me. "Be fast."

I took Gar with me so he wouldn't be in the way and went to Rollie's, the general store a mile down the road.

I left Gar in the car and hurried inside, making a small jump over the golden lab, Sunny Boy, sleeping in front of the door.

I looked around, but didn't see Enid, the store's owner.

"Thea, dear!" she called out to me.

I turned again as she appeared from the backroom. Today her long cardigan sweater was an outdoor scene. A baby blue sky with a bottom hem of green grass. Three dimensional clouds dotted the sky, and several flowers sprung up from the grass. It was a sweater my grandma would have adored.

"I have to make it fast," I told her as I pulled the list from my jeans' pocket. "Do you have any of these things?" I handed her the list.

She looked it over, shook her head, and handed it back. "Afraid not, dear."

I sighed. "Thanks. This cornhole thing is already a nightmare."

"I got my tickets!" She patted the pocket of her sweater. "I just love cornhole. You know, every year, Rollie and I would have a summer-long competition with your grandparents. Of course, Bettie and Jack always beat us."

"They did live near the cornhole courts. I bet they snuck in late-night practices all the time."

"Well, I never was that good at sports." She shrugged.

"I better get going before Nolan strangles Hugo."

I hugged her goodbye before bolting out the door.

I continued on the long trek into the main town of Branson, Missouri. The drive took over thirty minutes, and I had received four new text messages before I arrived, listing more items that Nolan needed to make things right for the competition.

I hurried through the building-supply store and sped all the way back, taking phone calls as I could to alleviate some of the chaos happening in the campground. When I returned in the early afternoon, it appeared as if a global disaster had broken out and hundreds of people had come to Cedar Fish Campground for refuge.

Cars, campers, and people spilled into every inch of the grounds. Inside the office, Sally struggled with the line while Curtis inched his way through the store aisles, helping people find things and answering questions. Nolan and Hennie were still with Hugo and Ray, but now more men had joined the gathering. One group stood directing the other.

Before I could talk to Nolan to get an update, Sally called on the walkie. "Umm, hello? Is anyone there? I need Thea?"

"You don't have to say hello every time, Sally. You can just start talking," I explained. Again.

"Sorry. I think there's a problem?"

"With?"

"Dill. The cat?"

"What's wrong with her?"

The last few weeks Dill had seemed slower and had slept more. I planned to take her to the vet if she quit eating, but that was the one thing she'd been doing just fine. Now, I felt the worry in the pit of my stomach again.

"I'm not sure. She's under your desk and she's panting and meowing funny."

"I'll be right there." I caught Hennie's eye from a distance and motioned for her to walk over. "Can you come with me a minute? Sally said something is wrong with Dill. You'll know better than me."

"Anything to get me away from these creeps," she said under her breath.

Gar bounded along with us. We found Sally in the back office, crying as she petted Dill. A long line of campers waited unhappily.

"Thanks, Sally. We'll take care of Dill if you can just help these campers, please?"

Sally nodded and wiped her eyes before returning to the front counter.

Hennie and I squatted down under the folding table I used as a desk and she looked Dill over. The tortoise-shell cat lay on her side, breathing fast and heavy, and let out a pained mew.

Hennie chuckled and tickled Dill's chin. "Old, rascally girl. Who knew you still had it? Oh, she's fine."

"She is?"

"I'd say within the next few hours, she'll be feeling much better."

"Why is—?"

Then Dill started to lick her back end fervently.

"I'd say she'll give birth within a few hours," Hennie said.

"Should I move her to my cabin?"

Hennie shook her head. "Better not disturb her like that. We'll close the door to give her privacy and she'll do just fine."

I put my hand to my forehead and reached for the travel mug of ice I'd left by my laptop that morning. "Any chance you want some kittens?"

"You've seen my menagerie. I'm not adding to that chaos."

Nolan crackled over the walkie, "I need help up here. What are you doing?"

"Checking on Dill. She's about to give birth."

There was a pause and then, "But she's not giving birth right now?"

"Nope, we're on our way. And we can add 'Find homes for kittens' to our task list because there's no way I'm having a litter running around this place."

"Fine. We have plenty of time to worry about that. Now get over here and get this moron off my back."

Get it here:

ZoeyChase.com/BreathOfFatalAir

About the Author

Zoey Chase received her MFA in creative writing from Carlow University. She lives in the Pittsburgh area with her husband, three daughters, three cats, and vast book collection. Can usually be found doing something bookish.

www.ZoeyChase.com
Facebook: /AuthorZoeyChase
Instagram: @AuthorZoeyChase

Made in USA - Kendallville, IN
1187983_9781951873011
10.30.2020 0920